ENDING RACISM IN THE CHURCH

ENDING RACISM IN THE CHURCH

Edited by

Susan E. Davies and
Sister Paul Teresa Hennessee, S.A.

United Church Press / Cleveland, Ohio

United Church Press, Cleveland, Ohio 44115

© 1998 by United Church Press

Paraphrase of Crossroads Ministry definition of racism and Principles of Institutional Change used by permission of Rev. Joseph R. Barndt. • Figure 1 reprinted by permission of Adrian van Kaam.

Biblical quotations, which have been adapted for inclusivity, are from the New Revised Standard Version of the Bible, © 1989 by the Division of Christian Education of the National Council of the Churches of Christ in the U.S.A., and are used by permission

Printed in the United States of America on acid-free paper

03   02   01   00   99   98   5   4   3   2   1

Library of Congress Cataloging-in-Publication Data

Ending racism in the church / edited by Susan E. Davies and
Sister Paul Teresa Hennessee.
     p.   cm.
     Includes bibliographical references.
     ISBN 0-8298-1238-5 (pbk. : alk. paper)
     1. Racism—Religious aspects—Christianity.   2. Racism—United
States—Case studies.   3. United States—Race relations—Case
studies.   I. Davies, Susan E.   II. Hennessee, Paul Teresa, 1935-   .
BT734.2.E53   1998
261.8'348'00973—dc21   98-20658
                                                                    CIP

CONTENTS

FOREWORD

As CHRISTIANS APPROACH the jubilee anniversary of the incarnation of Christ, they begin to examine their consciences as to how best to carry their fidelity forward into the third millennium. In the years of preparation for this great anniversary, one of the most important events will be the fiftieth anniversary Assembly of the World Council of Churches meeting in Harare, Zimbabwe, under the theme "Return to God, Rejoice in Hope" (1998). Leviticus 25 gives us some guidance in this call to conversion and celebration. The people of Israel were challenged to a sabbatical year in which justice would be restored in the land and the relations among peoples would be brought back into the order that would mirror God's will for peace and justice. As we stand on the threshold of the year 2000 and prepare for the World Council Assembly, we are challenged to examine what more can be done to realize the unity Christ prayed for among his disciples, and to root out the sins of our people, the sin of racism among them.

This volume provides a diverse series of essays and case studies that may contribute to any Christian community that studies them in equipping them in their common witness to the church's mission to eradicate the sin of racism in the society and in the churches. In reading these essays, the reader will find a wide range of viewpoints, occasionally contradicting, more often complementing one another. The book itself is a witness to the diversity and urgency of the struggle against racism and against all factors that divide Christ's church.

We pray that readers and the churches in which they serve may be renewed and revived in the spiritual life by reading and discussing these essays. The churches have made some contributions to the struggle against racism, yet they are challenged ever to do more in response to God's free grace in Jesus Christ. Steps toward the unity of the church have been significant, but the pilgrimage has many stages before it. We pray that these next years, as we reflect on the jubilee call of the gospel, might be particularly productive times of repentance and reconciliation in response to Christ's call "that they all may be one."

Bishop Melvin Talbert, President
National Council of Churches of Christ in the USA

Bishop Curtis Guillory, Chair
National Conference of Catholic Bishops'
Committee on African American Catholics

Konrad Reiser, General Secretary
World Council of Churches

PREFACE

THE WORK THAT PRODUCED THIS BOOK began in 1989 among a small group of ecumenical scholars and community activists who were completing a collection of essays on AIDS as an issue that divides the church. We were and are part of a larger movement known as Faith and Order, which has as its fundamental commitment the visible unity of the church of Jesus Christ throughout the globe.

Our study group has for the last fifteen years operated on an action/reflection model in which we consciously move previously marginalized issues or people to the center of theological work. We all know, for instance, that because AIDS first occurred in the United States among Haitians and gay men, the disease was—and to some extent still is—treated as the judgment of God on a subgroup or despised minority. Thus, we moved AIDS to the center and looked at how theology and the unity of the church were altered by that shift. *The Church with AIDS,* edited by Letty Russell, was published in 1990.

We began plans for our next work by discussing how race functions as a church-dividing or a church-uniting issue, and we decided to use ourselves as the subject of the study. We were leery of taking up this painful subject for many reasons. The African American members of the group lived daily, hourly with the internal and external divisions caused by racism within the church in the United States. They were not at all sure that the white members of the group were engaging in anything other than politically correct dilettantism and doubted whether the white members had sufficient commitment to the subject to make it worth their energies. In addition, some African American members of the group were not convinced that writing one more article or publishing one more book would do anything other than satisfy the egos or professional needs of the authors while the book gathered dust on the shelves of distributors or well-meaning purchasers.

The white members of the group also had a variety of reasons for hesitation. White liberal guilt infected many of them. Would their overt and covert racism be directly challenged? Would they have to look too closely at themselves and be forced to admit the ways in which they perpetuated white racism in the church? Would they be personally attacked or ridiculed by others in the group as they struggled to confront the causes and effects of racism? Would they be able to hang in there through the painful sessions? Would the group as a whole be able to name the ways in which racism structured their own interactions? Could they even see the ways in which racism is built into the theology and history, the biblical interpretations and the very institutional structures of the church? If and when they saw, would they be willing to act, to face others and name and change the structures of racism in the church and in our society? Or would they simply lapse back into white privilege and give up the task before it was adequately begun?

When we began, the group was composed of African American, Chinese American, Hispanic American, and European American representatives of nine denominations. During the seven years of our work, we evolved into a group composed of African Americans and European Americans, and thus decided to concentrate on the ways in which North American racism affects relationships between those groups. We were clear that our discussions and writings had to correlate with our own experiences, and that the weight of the study was not to fall on the black members of the group. We intended to function on the principle that we were all people of color; the issue at hand was not the "nonwhites," that is, the "deviations" from the norm, but how "whiteness" functions in the United States as a church-uniting/church-dividing issue. We were looking for clues to understanding church unity and division when the experience of those who have been placed on the fringes is placed in the center of the theological circle.

The work of this study group has overlapped the Faith and Order quadrennia. We began the work on racism on a case study basis in 1989, presenting to one another situations in which we had been involved that were designed to combat racism in the church or the larger society. We read books such as the *Autobiography of Malcolm X* and, using the study group as a working document, engaged in a "Dismantling Racism" workshop led by Joe Agne and Dr. Iva Carruthers.

We found continually that only some members of the group did their "homework" between our semiannual gatherings, and that most of us were dragging our feet in a variety of ways. Anne Scheibner's case study in this volume documents some of that process.

In 1991, the group was reconstituted for the next Faith and Order quadrennium. Some members had completed their service as denominational representatives, and some moved to different study groups. New members were invited to join the work. For at least one of the Faith and Order meetings, we had serious doubts about whether enough individuals would join us to make a viable working group. Eventually, we were composed of five continuing members, of whom two were African Americans and three were European Americans, as well as eight new members, all African Americans. Whereas the group about whom Scheibner did her case study was largely European American, the group that has produced this book was largely African American.

Among the newly constituted group were African Americans of the historic black churches, the mainline Protestant churches, and the Roman Catholic Church. The group also included European Americans of mainline and Roman Catholic churches. In both groups were ordained female and male clergy as well as laity (two members of different religious congregations), theologians, pastors, professors, community workers, and ecumenical staff persons.

The focus of our work shifted from ourselves as a working document to the production of a book addressing racism as a church-dividing/church-uniting issue. While moving the focus from people to product was an apparently safer way to work, we still found ourselves struggling with one another and with the design of our product. Sister Paul Teresa Hennessee speaks to some of her personal hesitation during this time in her chapter. Nevertheless, we labored with and challenged one another continually.

The cochairs for six of the seven years of this work were a black man and a white woman, making intentional connections across gender and racial lines. (The final year was cochaired by the editors of this book, an African American and a European American.) The social structures of racism and sexism complicated this leadership and made the group even more aware of the importance of our work. We found that our personal histories with one another and the subject at hand made our common work even more difficult, giving us yet another example of the ways in which racism divides groups and disrupts the renewal of community.

Fortunately, communication within the group was good, and the struggles for dominance and power as well as the differing modes of leadership were pointed out and openly discussed. Tension between personalities was not long-lived because we were learning to be honest with one another and because we recognized that the enemy without was greater than the struggles among us. Indeed, we came to the point of wondering whether spiritual opposition to our task might be operative. We attended to our resistances and sought to understand more about the workings of racism within.

This volume on the eradication of racism is designed not only for those in church administrative positions but also and importantly for those of us in the pews who are most often the initiators of change. Our hope is that this offering can be a bridge between these two all-important groups of Christians who very often exchange places. Our plan is to engage the reader, and the groups to which you belong, in a conscious and deep journey toward the eradication of racism. Christian unity cannot exist with the sort of separation racism imposes.

THE EDITORS EXPRESS our gratitude to the members of Faith and Order, particularly our colleagues on the Unity and Renewal Study Group, for their honest and faithful work as well as their support of our editorial efforts. Norm Hjelm, director of Faith and Order during the development of this work, was particularly encouraging to our group in the stickier moments. Finally, without the steady support and nimble fingers of Elaine Keenan, the manuscript would never have reached its final stages in a timely fashion.

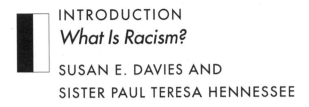

INTRODUCTION
What Is Racism?

SUSAN E. DAVIES AND
SISTER PAUL TERESA HENNESSEE

RACISM BEGINS WITH A BELIEF that race exists. Several of the authors in this volume challenge that belief, as do many modern scientists who hold that the concept has no basis in physical science. Race is a social construct, which some have traced to the period of European imperial expansion during the fifteenth century. "Prejudice" results when an individual or group holds that some races are by nature superior to others. Racial discrimination based on the belief of racial superiority is "bigotry." "Racism," then, is the abuse of power by a "racial" group that is more powerful than one or more other groups in order to exclude, demean, damage, control, or destroy the less powerful groups. Racism confers benefits upon the dominant group that include psychological feelings of superiority, social privilege, economic position, or political power.

The Minnesota Churches' Anti-Racism Initiative (chap. 1) proposes a helpful definition: racism equals race prejudice plus power. "Institutional racism" is the application of these beliefs and behaviors, consciously or unconsciously, in the structure, practices, and overt or hidden assumptions of an organization. "Cultural racism" is the application of these beliefs and practices in the mores, standards, customs, norms, language, and group life of a society. "White privilege," another term used in this volume, derives its descriptive power from the psychological feelings and institutional realities of the superiority, social privilege, economic position, and political power in the United States of European Americans.

The term "people of color" as a referent for persons in "racial" groups other than white has been directly and acutely challenged by Burton Tan, who declares that the term itself "implies a two-strata relationship; one, the 'people'; the other, the affixed and subordinated one of the 'of color.' The single term . . . 'people' refers to the white speakers and all the others are only referred [to] by an affixion or subordination." He draws a connection between "people of color" and other currently politically correct terms such as "persons with disabilities" and "people of different cultures." Hidden within the language, he rightly points out, is the assumption that white or North American or temporarily able-bodied people are the norm, and all others are deviations who need "'special treatment' after or different from the norm." He makes his point with a telling turn of phrase: Who are the "people of white"?[1]

ENDING RACISM IN THE CHURCH

As the foreword indicates, both national and international church leaders are committed to the eradication of racism within Christian circles or, as Rena Karefa-Smart puts it, committed to a nonracial future for the church. This book by itself will not eliminate racism. The working group recognizes that the hearts and minds of a majority of church members in the United States will not suddenly be transformed. Our hope, however, is that this book will raise consciousness of the insidious presence of racism within the structures and theologies of the church, and thereby move some Christians to anti-racist action.

This book offers a remarkable convergence of views from a wide spectrum of denominational perspectives. Not many volumes offer an academically based Presbyterian discussing baptism and a Pentecostal evangelist discussing the eucharist, both of whom argue from the authority of the biblical text while using it in vastly different ways. Similarly, two Church of God in Christ scholars and a Moravian bishop Christian Scriptures' scholar argue with and against the authority of the biblical text and the history of its interpretation in this book. We hope that persons within various traditions and across the denominations will be able to use these materials for vigorous conversation.

We have intentionally left the corners unrounded. For example, a wide range of theological and ecclesiological perspectives is reflected in differing language for God and different biblical texts. The language of the King James Version occupies a central place in the spiritual and communal life of many black churches, and this version is cited and quoted in several chapters.

Case Studies

The chapters that make up this book are arranged in three parts. Each part begins with a case study of groups of Christians who have engaged in the work of eradicating racism. The first study, for example, tells the story of developing antiracism teams to work in and through the churches of Minnesota. These teams aim to strengthen both understanding and action in the work of combating racism within local congregations and their regional structures, to "help churches become truly anti-racist multiracial communities." They work with a long-range, thirty-year vision that explicitly recognizes the embedded and intransigent nature of the racism infecting North American culture and congregations.

The second case study presents four separate programs that are offered to organizations, educational institutions, and individuals within the Milwaukee, Wisconsin, area. In both the Minnesota and the Wisconsin contexts, nonconfrontational approaches have proved the most productive in engaging European American people in anti-racism work. Both find that previously white congregations of urban, suburban, and rural plains states are being offered opportunities to learn with and from the increasingly pluralistic contexts in which they live.

The third case study moves in a different direction. Anne Scheibner, a white woman, seeks to understand the effect of racism in the life of our Unity and Renewal Study Group from 1989 to 1991. Her study offers a telling dissection of the ways in which a well-intentioned group can become ensnared in the coils of racist behaviors. The study details her progress toward living within the truth that "white racial identity cannot be made all right, nor can group distinctions based on race ever be made nice or comfortable. There is one race, and that is the human race. In Christ there is neither black nor white."

Flow of Parts and Chapters

The three parts move from descriptions of the ways racism functions in our individual and ecclesiastical lives, through materials that hold up new biblical and sacramental models for our common lives, to considerations of the historical and conciliar anti-racism work.

Chapter 2 offers Jack W. Hayford's confessional call to a transethnic church growing out of the change required of us by God. His chapter is a much shortened revision of his address to the 1995 Convention of the National Association of Evangelicals, in which, as a white man, he called the pentecostal movement to move beyond the racial divisions that so painfully separated that body. His chapter is particularly important because the Pentecostal Fellowship of North America was willing to go out of existence in 1995 to make way for the fully interreligious Pentecostal and Charismatic Fellowship of North America.

Leonard Lovett, an African American in the Church of God in Christ, argues in chapter 3 that racism is "the perverse worship of the self, rooted in spiritual pride," and calls upon both European American and African American Christians to build interracial bridges of understanding through repentance, humility, prayer, and action.

In chapter 4, Susan Davies of the United Church of Christ speaks of her difficulty, as a European American, of unearthing racism when living within an apparently monocultural context. She also offers an example of an educational process that can lead to combating racism.

Part 2 begins with a journey through the Christian Scriptures, as Arthur Freeman argues (in chapter 6) that only God can determine inclusion. As a European American and a Moravian bishop, he warns us that human beings adopt a fearful arrogance when we seek to create limits where God has refused to do so.

Alonzo Johnson draws in chapter 7 on the life and work of Howard Thurman to confront racism as a crisis of the human spirit. As an African American member of the Church of God in Christ, he gives particular attention to the work of Howard Thurman and the embodiment of a nonracial vision in the Church for the Fellowship of All Peoples in San Francisco.

In chapter 8, Deborah Mullen examines the theological nature of baptism. She concludes that racially based separation among Christians violates the fundamental nature of our unity in Christ. An African American Presbyterian, she calls all of us to "live as though our baptism has meaning in our daily lives."

Similarly, Tee Garlington, an African American Pentecostal evangelist, surveys in chapter 9 the grounding of the eucharist in both biblical testaments. She argues that "if we practice sectarianism or racism in any way, we are limiting our revelation, and we are hurting the whole body of Christ."

Sister Paul Teresa Hennessee in chapter 10 connects the work of Father Adrian van Kaam on Formative Spirituality with the origins of racism within individuals and communities. Hennessee, an African American Roman Catholic, maintains that violence and racism deny the presence of God within both the hater and the object of the hatred.

Part 3 moves into the recent history of the ecumenical movement and the ways in which work toward a nonracial church has been both promoted and frustrated in global and North American contexts. In chapter 12, Raymond Blanks reminds us of our need for conversion, based in the covenant of God with the people of God. As an African American, he challenges the church to renewed commitment and change.

Rena Karefa-Smart of the Episcopal Church offers in chapter 13 a vision of a nonracial church growing out of her experience with the Programme to Combat Racism of the World Council of Churches. An African American who grew up in the African Methodist Episcopal Church, she calls the churches to intentional koinonia communion lived on the other side of Christian racism.

Brother Jeffrey Gros is a European American Roman Catholic with long experience in the ecumenical movement. He looks in chapter 14 at the work of historic black churches within and alongside the ecumenical movement as well as the significance of international ecumenical dialogue in developing ways to undo racism.

The last element of this book is A Guide to Address Racism and Work for Justice (developed by the Center for Vision and Policy in Maine). The guide outlines six multimedia sessions so that groups can examine their own practices as well as those of their community. These sessions can be used over a six-week period or developed into a weekend retreat.

Study and Discussion Questions

Each chapter concludes with a series of questions designed for use in a study group or for personal reflection. The questions address individuals and communities, congregations and regional church bodies. Together with the case studies, the questions are intended to ground this book in the concrete reality of Christian life and faith. It is our hope that this book will find use in widely diverse congregations.

PART 1

Uncovering Racism in Churches

1 CASE STUDY:
Minnesota Churches' Anti-Racism Initiative
LOUIS SCHOEN

MINNESOTA EXPERIENCED a significant and rapid increase in racial diversity during the final third of the twentieth century. Demographic polarization grew still more rapidly, generally following patterns well established in other regions. During the century preceding the 1980s, seeing a Minnesotan of other than European ancestry outside the Twin Cities metropolitan area was an extremely rare, highly localized, and often temporary event—except on or near one of the thirteen Native American reservations scattered throughout most of the state.

An ever-growing metro suburban fringe remains almost exclusively European American. Inner suburbs experience growing diversity, but most persons of African, Asian, Latin American, or indigenous ancestry live in the inner cities of Minneapolis and Saint Paul, with smaller clusters in the cities of Duluth, Rochester, Saint Cloud, and Moorhead. By the early 1990s, students of European descent had become a minority in Minneapolis public schools.

During the 1980s and 1990s, racial "diversity" has reached a number of smaller, rural communities, mostly following one of two patterns: (1) educational institutions recruited a diverse student body, often beginning with athletes; or (2) agribusinesses recruited low-wage workers from the Texas border region or among refugees resettled in Minnesota. In both situations, the schools or businesses did little to prepare the wider community to accept and appreciate racial/ethnic diversity, and the emerging residential distribution—especially of low-wage workers—typically followed ghettoized patterns familiar in urban centers. Latent white racism, previously concealed by European American homogeneity, often has frustrated efforts to address other social concerns emerging in these communities.

By far the largest ethnic groups that settled in Minnesota, after Anglo-Saxons consolidated European power in the region, originated in Germany and Scandinavia. Reflecting these demographics, most Minnesota Christians traditionally were Lutheran or Roman Catholic. More than two-thirds of all church members remain about evenly divided between these two faith groups. Church structures located entirely within the state include six Catholic dioceses and six synods of the Evangelical Lutheran Church in America (ELCA). The Lutheran Church Missouri Synod (LC-MS) also is a profound influence.

THE MINNESOTA COUNCIL OF CHURCHES

During an era in which state councils of churches and their denominational members alike have been declining in size, strength, and community influence—and some state councils have been dissolved—the Minnesota Council of Churches (MCC) has thrived. It was managed through a severe financial crisis in the mid-1980s without losing member support. It continues to operate significant programs of service, advocacy, education, and dialogue as well as an office building that houses six denominational offices and twenty-three church-related agencies in addition to its own ministries. The council remains a respected voice in public affairs although the role of religion in public life has declined, here as elsewhere, amidst the escalating secularism and hedonism in U.S. culture.

Until 1998, the Minnesota Council of Churches consisted of eighteen denominational judicatories: the six ELCA synods, four Presbyteries (two of them interstate jurisdictions), the statewide Episcopal Diocese and Conferences of the United Church of Christ and United Methodist Church, and the smaller Congregational Fellowship, plus Minnesota units of interstate judicatories of the Christian Church (Disciples of Christ), Church of the Brethren, Mid-American Baptist, and Moravian Churches. The Minnesota Catholic Conference has observer status only but supports joint public policy advocacy with the Minnesota Council of Churches and the Jewish Community Relations Council.

BACKGROUND

Some MCC judicatories, historically or recently, have maintained ministries among Minnesotans of Latin, African, Asian, or Native American descent. Primarily African American denominations historically have not been part of the Minnesota Council of Churches even though some have as many churches in Minnesota as some MCC judicatories. An exception: the Church of God in Christ was a member for several years but withdrew in 1992 for reasons never officially stated, although there were allusions to "theological differences." Some local African American church leaders indicated preference for involvement in the urban-oriented, congregationally based Greater Minneapolis and Saint Paul Area Councils of Churches (GMCC and SPACC).

The Minnesota Council of Churches is officially motivated by the basic vision of Christian ecumenism. It is constitutionally self-defined as "a community of communions who confess Jesus Christ as Lord and Savior," which "seeks to manifest within the State of Minnesota the unity of the Church in Christ." Its broad strategy is stated in this way: "Relying on the transforming power of the

Holy Spirit, the Council works to bring its members into life-giving fellowship and into common witness, study and action in the glory of God and in service to all creation."

The dissonance between this vision and the more limited ecumenical reality was widely recognized but rarely acknowledged openly until the mid-1990s.

Following the 1992 Simi Valley decision and South Central Los Angeles insurrection, a renewal of focus and energy emerged for work against racism in the Minnesota Council of Churches, the Greater Minneapolis Council of Churches, and the Saint Paul Area Council of Churches, as in many other groups. Most denominations and some congregations had some form of anti-racism work under way, some of long standing, with varying effectiveness. The GMCC and SPACC Ecumenical Partners programs and MCC ethnic ministries had achieved important gains in behalf of their constituencies and identified some critical underlying needs.

Staff members, executives, or program committees had spoken out publicly against overtly racist incidents and practices. Educational events had been planned to demythologize the "Columbus discovery" quincentennial and to highlight the racism inherent in U.S. history. The councils were among resources for local justice groups which, at the 1991 World Series and 1992 Super Bowl in Minneapolis, protested professional sports franchises' abuse of the identities of Native American nations and tribes.

The Los Angeles events added urgency and focus to the work under way. Inspired by the book *Dismantling Racism: The Continuing Challenge to White America* by Joseph R. Barndt (Augsburg, 1991), MCC staff began strategizing toward a more structured programmatic approach. It began with recognition of three realities:

1. There are widespread, often conflicting differences in basic understanding of what racism is and how it influences human behavior.
2. Effective action against racism requires collective effort including interracial collaboration.
3. Working together against racism is impossible without common understanding of what we are opposing.

PARADIGM

Here is a dictionary definition of racism:

1. A belief in the inherent superiority of a particular race and its right to domination over others. 2a. A doctrine or political program based on the assumption of racism and designed to execute its principles. b. A political or social system founded on racism.[1]

To distinguish systemic racism (definition 2) from personal prejudice, Barndt uses the following formula:[2]

$$Racism = Race\ prejudice + (the\ systemic\ abuse\ of)\ Power.$$

Institutional racism applies these beliefs and behaviors, consciously or unconsciously, in the structure, practices, and overt or hidden assumptions of an organization. Cultural racism applies them in the mores, standards, norms, language, religion, and group life of a society. Personal prejudice is empowered and perpetuated in these cultural and institutional forms. They facilitate and encourage denial of racism by its perpetrators as well as projection upon its objects of the blame for racism's social manifestations.

Race itself, Barndt observes, "is an arbitrary socio/biological classification created by Europeans (white men), during the time of worldwide colonial expansion, to assign human worth and social status, using themselves as the model of humanity, for the purpose of legitimizing white power and white skin privilege."[3]

Barndt's elaboration has been especially influential: he underlines three primary power dynamics that support race prejudice when expressed in cultural and institutional racism in the United States. The power of racism (1) grants special, largely unrecognized privileges and power to white people, (2) oppresses persons of color and imposes internalized victimization, and (3) imprisons all members of the society in a racist system that has "ultimate power to control and destroy everyone."[4]

Such complex, systemic evil impairs our ability to recognize the redemptive power of Christ in its application to the human sphere. If we cannot confess complicity in so great a sin, how can we hope for forgiveness and reconciliation? This spiritual struggle is vital to an understanding of the church's role in confronting cultural and institutional oppression and in challenging the church to confront itself.

PRINCIPLES OF INSTITUTIONAL CHANGE

Barndt offers six principles of institutional change that have been adopted as basic assumptions in the MCC anti-racism work.[5] They are paraphrased here.

1. The task is organizing for systemic change. The institution must be equipped with new expectations of racial justice.
2. The New Testament model is an anti-racist multiracial community. This implicitly recognizes that it is not enough for white Americans to try to be nonracist. In a pervasive racist system that empowers them, this is impossible. Furthermore, building diverse, multicultural communities is an unrealistic aim when approached without addressing racism. If white skin color re-

mains an empowering stamp of privilege in a racially diverse community, it is a racist multiracial community.

3. The accountability for change in the church belongs to members. It is an inside job. Institutional endorsement is required as a fundamental step. The effort must be affirmed, endorsed, called, sent. Working for institutional change from outside the institution can never bring truly fundamental changes. If external actions are necessary to gain the institution's attention, parallel internal efforts, with other visible leadership, are necessary in order to build lasting change.

4. An effective model for change must be tailor-made to the institution, keyed to its language and structure. In the church, it must be faith-based, living out the gospel.

5. The strategy utilized is to build trained, equipped leadership teams, discerning and building skills of analysis, strategizing, education, and organizing.

6. Institutional tranformation requires long-range planning. A thirty-year vision frames the current year's goals. The aim of team members is to begin the work of institutionalizing anti-racism as an overt, visible aspect of the church's identity—and to build a system for replacing themselves.

7. Your church is not alone—in the world or spiritually. In working for change, spiritual emphasis must be fundamental and pervasive, but not isolating. The task includes community, societal change, with explicit accountability to the communities of color that racism oppresses.

STRATEGY

The overall strategy reflects wisdom expressed by Danny Duncan Collum:

> If we are serious about expunging racism, at least from American public life, we will have to start simultaneously at the bottom and the top. At the top we need clear signals from political, religious and cultural leaders that racism is unAmerican, un-Christian, unacceptable. At the bottom we need a genuine attempt to understand the forces that lead frightened and insecure white people into the racist trap, and a new politics that can unite people of all races around what are, for the most part, shared grievances and aspirations.[6]

The strategy was to develop a group of ecumenical anti-racism teams to work in and through the churches of Minnesota. The aim was to include strengthening both local church and denominational efforts against racism. Teams of skilled educators and organizers would be developed to help churches become truly anti-racist multiracial communities. Starting with a Consultation on Racism, September 18, 1992, the Minneapolis Council of Churches facilitated the development of a vision and structure for a broad-based anti-racism initiative by Minnesota church communities. Recognizing no ready-made models in place, the council contracted Barndt's assistance in developing one. His cotrainer in intensive seminars was Barbara Major, also associated with the People's Institute for Survival and Beyond of New Orleans.

The Minnesota Churches' Anti-Racism Initiative (MCARI) was created by a Planning and Design Team with participation from most MCC member judicatories as well as from the African Methodist Episcopal and National Baptist traditions, Minnesota Roman Catholic dioceses, and the Greater Minneapolis and Saint Paul Area Councils of Churches. Some participants had evangelical, pentecostal, or independent traditions.

A three-phase, coordinated developmental program was undertaken. Phase 1 was comprised of the planning and design work. It set out to achieve initial ownership, preliminary funding, affirmations or endorsements, assignments for participants, and an evaluation system. After six months' preparation and a two-month implementation process, the Minnesota Churches' Anti-Racism Initiative was adopted in June 1993 for resourcing and coordination as a program of the Minnesota Council of Churches. Phase 1 ended with formal MCC board action to sponsor the initiative.[7] Identification of potential partners for racial justice also began during this phase and continues today.

Phase 2 trained eighty-seven persons and formed eight regional anti-racism teams to work in all areas of the state, to analyze the dynamics of racism within church institutions, to prioritize anti-racism work, and to begin to discern more clearly how we can join others in the struggle for racial justice. This phase may be repeated indefinitely into the future in a process of team expansion and renewal.

Phase 3, the strategy and action phase, is ongoing, but it begins with advanced training. Three one-day organizing workshops were provided for the entire team; 27 members developed their anti-racism educational skills in a four-day seminar, and 10 others attained similar in-depth organizing skill-training. By July 1995, the team had conducted 77 educational events in 44 Minnesota communities for 1,662 participants from 283 congregations and 66 other organizations. Thirty team members had served as facilitators and 23 as organizers and hosts.

The long-range goal is to dismantle institutional racism within the church and, working through the churches, to counteract racism in society. Teams begin by identifying needs, strengths, and opportunities, looking for "open doors" within existing practices and power structures. They offer educational services and will examine mission, goals, objectives, structures, priorities, and actions. They seek to help churches and related groups to listen more systematically to the voices of people of color and to develop plans and strategies to build greater inclusiveness and power sharing.

Initial targets for in-depth institutional analysis were the Minnesota, Greater Minneapolis, and Saint Paul Area Councils of Churches. This analysis has proceeded since 1995 within a new administrative structure that combines resources of the three councils to support and staff anti-racism work.[8] It led to a personal initiative by MCC Executive Director Peg Chamberlin, which attracted in 1998, as the council's nineteenth member, the historical and black Minnesota State Baptist Convention.

The initiative affirms: Our mission, which we enter into prayerfully and with God's help, is:

- to activate a reconciliation process which will be both confessional and healing;
- to commit our energy and resources to dismantle institutional racism in our denominations/congregations;
- to release the grip of racism within our families and individual lives; and
- to become a healthy influence in order to transform our Christian institutions into authentic multiracial, anti-racist communities.

LEARNINGS AND IMPLICATIONS

Structural Learning

A model now is in place, capable of replication or adaptation elsewhere to guide development of collective anti-racism programming in the church. Most dimensions apply to denominational as well as ecumenical initiatives. The Minnesota Churches' Anti-Racism Initiative in 1997 began focusing on development of congregational anti-racism teams as its primary emphasis.

Strategic Learning

Recruiting people willing to undergo the intensive, three-day initial training and to make the commitment to ongoing team participation remains a challenge. Staff and team members are testing new approaches to promotion and rhetorical framing of the work without sacrificing its principles. In an era when mass media quickly popularize, typecast, and then destroy or discard words and concepts over short periods of time, being adaptable and creative in communicating with a wide audience is vital.

Paradigmatic Learning

Some studies suggest that the natural human state, reflected in small children until adult influences change them, is marked by egalitarian, value-neutral perception of all who are "other" than the self. Prejudice and self-hatred alike are taught, overcoming natural instincts. Socialization into a system of oppression, whether of perpetrators or victims, relies upon acceptance of cognitive dissonance. As people grow in understanding of social norms, in awareness of how relationships and community work best in comparison with how they are, functional dissonance occurs as well. As people learn basic faith teachings, in relation to institutional religious behavior, they experience spiritual dissonance. The mind is highly sensitive, however, to evidence of disparate power relationships and can be molded by systems of authority to accept dissonance as normative.

The system is supported and the dissonance overcome by power and privilege granted to one group and the threat of punishment or deprivation imposed upon another. In the socialization of oppressors, unspoken messages of educators, popular media, business and government, and many churches include the following:

It is a dangerous world.
Prejudice is a necessary aspect of personal security.
Dissonance is normal.
Resolving dissonance requires accepting the system and your status.
Accountability for power is necessarily ambiguous.
Change is impossible.

Persons who hold economic, social, and political power as an elite class unavoidably experience their self-interest bound up in perpetuating these myths and preserving the status quo.

The grace of God is first experienced by an oppressor in a challenging confrontation, a demand for confession, repentance, and liberation. Only then are forgiveness and reconciliation possible. The spiritual dissonance must be confronted and proclaimed, and the steps initiated to resolve it before the hope can be claimed for personal redemption and for social and institutional change.

QUESTIONS

1.   Does your church participate in the regional or state Council of Churches? Have you ever had direct contact with the staff of the state council? Do you know what its programs are? How might you learn more about the ecumenical work being done by your regional council?

2.   What anti-racism work has been done in your region? In your community? Are there trained leaders in your area who could help you develop a program similar to the one described? The local Peace and Justice Center and the Council of Churches usually have contact with such trained leaders.

3.   When did you first notice the cognitive and spiritual dissonance described in this case study? How might you help address those dissonances in your congregation's educational programs?

2 | *Confessing What Separates Us*

JACK W. HAYFORD

THE APOSTLE PAUL SAID, "I was not disobedient to the heavenly vision" (Acts 26:19). As he made his proclamation to King Agrippa, Paul described something that was experientially based and biblically sound and founded. I want to talk about a heavenly vision. I believe it is a heavenly vision for this hour, for this time, when God is saying to the church, "The only way you are going to make your message credible to the world and penetrate the opportunities for evangelism of the hour is for there to come together a disappearance of those things that have separated you." We call it "racism"; I call it the absence of trans-ethnicity.

ONLY ONE RACE—THE HUMAN RACE

Our very use of the words "racism" and "racial division" is in itself a reflection of the horrendous degree to which racial attitudes have become entrenched in and engraved upon our systems. Properly speaking, a believer in Jesus Christ should never speak of racial differences for the simple biblical reason that the Bible specifically says there is only one race. That revelation is not anything I need to argue. All of us know it: God "has made from one blood every nation of men to dwell on all the face of the earth" (Acts 17:26 NKJV). Jesus did not come to die for the races of the world. He came to die for the race of Adam and Eve.

The fact that we have so many differences essentially stems from what happened at Babel where human pride sought to mount up with arrogance before God. As a result, there came the dissemination of the peoples of the world through that awful separation of Babel. Arrogance and pride occasioned the judgment. The outflow of it was not just the inconvenience of various languages, but the establishment of the cultural differences or the ethnicities that separate peoples. That is, whenever we deal with ethnic barriers, we deal with something that was the result of human sin and pride.

Separation, Human Pride, and the Tower of Babel

Two implications are central. First, from a theological perspective, more cultural influences separate me and my attitudinal stance toward other ethnic groups than I am willing to acknowledge. To whatever degree that I fail to acknowledge this, I surrender to the impact of the same pride that brought the separation at Babel—no matter to what degree grace or sanctification has had its process in my personal life of holiness and growth and understanding and love of Christ.

Second, from a social perspective, all persons are racist. Such social definition does not imply that we are hostile and belligerent people who burn crosses, shoot people, or mount campaigns of bitter discrimination. Socially, what divides us is an unconscious fear that has laid hold of us.

PERSONAL EXPERIENCE

I want you to walk a path with me as I go back to my experiences as a young pastor. I was raised in Oakland, California. If you are familiar with that city, you know that today it is largely an African American community. In the years of my upbringing, the African American community was much smaller. Even so, I was raised in an environment that was more integrated than other parts of the nation during that time. No one should be smug because of her or his environment. But being raised in an integrated environment, I never thought of myself as being anything other than a generous, large-hearted American with regard to all racial groups.

Hidden Prejudice

In 1957, the first year of my pastorate, I began to recognize that I had hidden prejudice. Efforts were being made then to integrate Central High School in Little Rock. Anyone who was around at the time remembers that significant beginning point in our nation when a federal mandate to integrate the school was met with resistance.

The civil struggle and the national stir caused by this situation occasioned the radio commentary that I heard one day. I was listening to the radio as I worked in the basement of a tiny church in Indiana. My wife and I had recently planted the church, and I was building shelves for the storage of church school materials. I remember so clearly the electric moment that came to my experience of self-discovery that hour. About five in the afternoon, Sinclair Lewis, a well-known radio commentator at that time, was giving a commentary on what was happening in Little Rock. I heard him say something to the effect that it is impossible to have been raised in the twentieth-century United States and not be racially prejudiced.

As I was nailing the boards in place, I thought to myself, "That's not true!" I thought about my background in Oakland and said to myself, "I played basketball where there were blacks and whites together. I brought guys home with me for lunch who were African Americans. I'm not prejudiced!"

Then I heard God speak to me. I do not know how God speaks to you. Without elaboration, I will simply say that God spoke to me. God said to me while I was in that tiny church basement, "Yes, Jack, you are. Yes, you are prejudiced." Then the Holy Spirit brought pictures to my mind's eye, as though a videotape was being played before me. I saw not one picture, but a composite. It wasn't that faces were ushered before me, but it revealed a practice I had that was racially based. I felt the shame of self-discovery at that moment as I realized, "Sovereign God, I didn't see that about myself."

God was dealing with me about my inner reaction. The picture was this: whenever I would shake hands with a person who was black, I had a feeling that my hand was not clean afterward. Now there is no question that I knew better. I had never even allowed this to register in my conscious mind to the degree that I saw my need to repent and said, "You know, I need to get over that way of thinking." But all of a sudden God was saying, "Yes, you are. You are prejudiced." And the picture was there, revealing to me an unrecognized feeling. I realized that when I shook hands, I always felt as if something had been deposited on my hand. But that feeling was there. The existence of that feeling, cultural difference, did not manifest itself in pride, hatred, or animosity. I did not feel anything other than so much different from, a separation that was suddenly unveiled before my heart's understanding. I did not know it until that moment.

I was a young pastor. I got on my knees there in that little room where I was working on the shelves and said, "Sovereign God, I didn't even know that existed. I don't know what I'm supposed to do with this information, God, but I ask you to forgive me and help me to always recognize that you help me with the things that would make my heart not be like yours."

Hidden Prejudice about the Civil Rights Movement

I did not know that what happened on that day would take me on a pathway that would eventually unfold more of my attitudes. They were not dramatic moments, but episodes that occurred to me as an evangelical believer. For example, I did not realize how blinded I was in my attitude toward the civil rights movement of the 1960s. By that time, I was working in the headquarters of our denominational offices. I was passive toward what was taking place in the black community that was seeking to establish its civil rights; I did not realize how that passivity was being read by my evangelical brothers and sisters in the black community.

I do not have any idea how many evangelicals marched at Selma or anyplace else like that. I know that nobody marched from any of the circles I was in. As a matter of fact, although I did not have any social commentary to make about it, I never did speak against what was going on. I had associates who suggested that Martin Luther King Jr. perhaps was not as godly a man as some thought. I had associates who suggested that he might be under Communist influence. I never heard anybody preach it from a pulpit in an evangelical church, and I certainly did not have any disposition to say anything that way myself. But I was really rather indifferent. It seemed safe just to say nothing and to do nothing.

Even though I never verbalized it, I am sorry to say that I felt somewhat superior to the liberal white pastors (who did not embrace the sound message of Jesus Christ and the true veracity of the Word of God with a fidelity of the inerrancy and the infallibility of the sacred scriptures—and all of those things that I held dear) who were marching for civil rights causes. I would think, "Oh, that's those liberals. That's all they've got to do. They are not interested in the spread of the gospel, so they just go down and march with the blacks for the sake of some political issue." I did not realize how deeply entrenched that way of thought was in me.

I was horribly arrogant as an evangelical just in regard to that smallness of mind toward others in the body of Christ who approached things differently from the way I did. Even if their doctrine was not something that met my specifications, there was no justification for my being so small-minded about who they were as human beings. (That, by the way, is something we in our evangelical tradition are remarkably capable of doing. And that is even within our circle of the evangelical community where we are spiteful in our attitudes toward one another—although we are courteous in the way we handle that separation. We can be incredibly mean in our hearts while being appropriately gracious in our public and social relationships.)

It is not because any one of us is mean of heart. This is not an indictment. We are schooled in this by our traditions, our culture. It could be our denominational culture or, in this case, the culture of our ethnicity, our society. It is an amazingly profound thing that we are able to tolerate this attitude in ourselves without recognizing it. Would we recognize it, we would be mad; we would have none of it because we are too committed to Jesus and the Word. But we do not perceive it in ourselves until there come moments of disclosure that only the Holy Spirit can bring us to if the Spirit can get our attention and if the Spirit can find in us a willingness to be changed. I detect that we are at a time when we are willing to say, "Let us be changed."

Do we have a willingness to be changed? Our response to that question could be, "Well, what do you mean, am I willing to be changed? About what? I don't see myself as in need of any particular change. I am as generous as I want to be." That is the point. All of the generosity that we have shown in terms of racial tolerance does not cut it. We are not going to get there apart from coming to some very severe places of confrontation like the point of my self-discovery.

Your point of self-discovery may not be the same as mine. I may be the sole sinner in regard to that confrontation with myself. When I would shake hands with a black person, I didn't think, "This is a dirty person." I knew better than that and would never have thought it consciously. But I still had the feeling, and I had to acknowledge it because with this feeling there was an absence of caring. I discovered years later that my brothers and sisters who were as evangelical as I was—my black brothers and sisters who were involved in the civil rights movement—thought that God had sent a prophet to their day. They thought that God was giving them a revival.

All the while, I was sitting passively by, feeling, "I'm not sure what I really think about this. But one thing I know, I'm not going to really do much of anything about it." Be discreetly quiet. Keep your distance. Why? Because at the bottom line, we had congregations that were not sure how to respond. We had to be sure that we did not alienate the support base. Well, is this a condemnation toward who we were thirty years ago or so? No, it is not. It is an acknowledgment of who we were.

We probably could not have been anything else because the self-discovery, the ability to navigate change, does not happen that fast in human nature. Some things break if we push them too fast. Rather, what we need to do is to move on toward healing. And so, we are at a time when it is important to acknowledge what we have not been in the past. This is not for the purpose of condemning the past, but for confronting the present in the light of the realities that the past has disclosed.

Blind Spots on My Soul

Now, I come to 1968 when I was doing graduate studies. I wrote a paper on the subject of miscegenation. I studied the background of some of the traditions in some sectors of the evangelical movement where there had been a purported theological, biblical base for the separation of the races—the so-called curse of Ham (Gen. 9:18–27; actually Canaan was cursed), which was taken as a warrant for separating the races and enslaving blacks. My whole paper demonstrated that the Word of God cannot be used to justify anything other than a full acceptance, a full embrace, of transethnic marriages. The paper went on to conclude safely, however—I wrote it from conviction—that in view of the cultural difficulties and the sociological separations and the problems that exist, the church might better avoid such transethnic marriages.

It was happening again, but I could not see it. Even though I was willing to accept the biblical viability of a transethnic marriage, I was so much enculturated in our traditions that I quickly built the walls back up by saying that probably it would be wisest not to marry transethnically. I expressed my views in my paper more thoroughly than I am doing now, but the whole point is that this is where I stood in 1968 on the issue. I still had blind spots in my soul.

The Requirements of Dominion Correctness

Then I came to my present pastorate at the Church on the Way in Van Nuys, California. The story of that development is a miracle story like the crossing of the

Red Sea. It was one of those times when God was doing a miracle, and I was privileged just to be in the middle of it.

As things unfolded in our church, I had no concept that what was happening would begin to change a whole body of my viewpoints. One of the first was the definition of success that I had as an evangelical pastor. I did not even realize how to define success. What was occurring in our church began to challenge the very thing that was defined in my mind as success in the evangelical tradition—a burgeoning, beautifully developed suburban church.

When I came to that pastorate more than twenty-five years ago, we were in a relatively suburban part of the city of Los Angeles in an area known as the San Fernando Valley. Since then, our demographics have changed radically. Now, we are almost entirely urban in our situation. The turning point in our perception took place when the church started to grow and we thought, "You know, we don't have enough room to grow here."

We looked around for twenty- to thirty-acre parcels of land farther out from the city in more suburban areas. As we looked for a place to go, there came one of the most profound dealings of God in my life and in the life of our congregation. God, by the Spirit, grabbed the elder-body of our church by the nape of the neck and sat us down. It was almost like that. To try to describe how that took place would take too long, but God stopped us and very plainly directed, "You are not to relocate." The direction came so clearly, and we were so awestruck in the reverence of God, that we knew to try to move would result in lost blessing. And so we stayed, not because of infighting or congregational resistance to moving, but because God said, "Don't move."

Staying where we were was inconvenient, but resolutions came that finally helped us to break out of the small box we were in. One was the opportunity to purchase the entire campus of the Van Nuys First Baptist Church a half mile away from us, which opened up possibility for development. We kept our current campus, which by then enveloped about ten acres. With the use of both campuses, we were given some elbowroom to be and to become without having to move away.

That dealing of God to remain in the city is pivotal to my being able to discuss this issue with you now. If we had moved ten, twelve, or fourteen miles away, I do not think I would have made additional points of self-discovery.

As the face of our immediate community began to change, I felt the need to sensitize our congregation to what it was becoming. I brought a message entitled "Outracing the World." In other words, we needed to outrace the way the world thinks. The message was that in a field of transethnicity, beyond integration is forgiveness, beyond toleration is Christlikeness, and beyond being politically correct is dominion correctness. As I set forth the message before the people, I said it was a message that was due to a divinely appointed decision made years earlier. That was the decision God put on us, "Do not move. Do not relocate."

God was awakening in us a growing sense of submission to what the Spirit was working in us.

I understand that basically is the place where many churches are right now. They have a sense of mission, but may not have noticed their communities. Here is God's message to you: if we are going to model to the world what Jesus raised up the church to be (in contrast to the world in its separatism) and if we are going to penetrate the urban centers of the world (nearly all of which are of a melting together of races), then we are going to have to learn to overcome some of the encrusted points of separation in our system. These are not points of bitter resistance, but unperceived points of separation that encrust themselves in our souls. Let us do something about it. This begins on a personal level. That is why I am giving you a personal testimony.

Race Blindness

My message is born out of several points of insight and self-discovery of my pastoral journey. Now I come to a point of fairly recent date. I had been on a nationally televised talk show. There was another person on the program with me, although he was interviewed separately on an entirely different subject. As we were going from the talk show to the airport, this person said, "I understand that [he named two people] are going to be married at your church. Are you going to be performing the ceremony?" I said, "Yes." To that, he replied, "Well, do you feel comfortable about their situation?"

I was not really sure what the person was referencing. He is fairly well known in his particular denominational circles, and I know him well enough. Not knowing for sure what he meant by "their situation," I said, "Well, yes, I think so." We separated at the airport, taking different airlines. On the way home, I thought, "Since this man is a personal friend of the family, I wonder if he knows something about that couple that I don't know." I was wondering if there was some earlier marital involvement that had not been disclosed to me in pastoral counsel.

Still feeling uneasy about his question, "Are you going to be performing the ceremony?" I thought I had better give him a call. When I reached him, I asked, "I hope this isn't awkward, but I got to thinking about your remark. What was it about their situation that concerned you and occasioned your asking me if I felt comfortable about performing their marriage?" He said, "Well, look, Jack, it's no really big deal. It was just that he's white and she's black."

Here was the thing that was so profoundly moving to me as I looked back on my life's journey. I had once written a graduate paper—and gotten an *A* on it— that the marriage of blacks and whites may not be socially practical, even though it is biblically sound to do so. Here I was giving counsel to a couple whose wedding I was performing in a few weeks, and it had not even entered my mind that she was black and he was white. Something had changed in me! I do not mean that I just ignored the difference. I mean that the difference did not register.

Incidentally, I discovered, and I wish it was not so, that our church has been a haven for some people in Los Angeles whose transethnic marriages were not accepted elsewhere. Nobody told these couples that they had to leave their churches, but their social relationships evaporated in their former churches. These people had not married out of spite in order to make a point or social statement. These people loved God, and they came to know each other and to love each other and love Christ and got married. And we accept them.

A PENTECOST CHURCH OF ALL NATIONS

At Pentecost, when the church was formed and the outpouring of God's Spirit took place, there was a call to the peoples of the earth. There was an announcement of the latter days that were to extend in intensity from then on forward. How much the world in these last days desperately needs a liberated people to preach the full liberating power of the gospel—to bring in the last days' harvest.

On that day of Pentecost, there were those who asked, "What does this mean?" Three thousand people came to Christ, and the Bible says that there were among them not only Jews (which in itself would have been an ethnic sector from at least twelve different nations) but proselytes as well. Acts 2 specifically says that people had come from a number of Gentile traditions. The church was born with a dominion of grace that began with God demonstrating the Spirit's power to people from all parts of the earth, saying, "This is what I'm wanting to do from the onset of the church."

The church has not been good at doing that consistently. I know that as an evangelical in North America, I have not been very good at doing it for much of my life. We have not been very good at modeling that. We have lived out more the cultural system in terms of this particular facet of life than what the Bible reveals to us was God's desire at the very onset of our founding.

As we seek to find how to move forward and be different from the culture in this very difficult area, we need not berate ourselves because of the way things were, or the way we were, in the past. In these last days, we need to confront those things and say, "We can't live that way anymore. It is not an hour in which it can be allowed." We need to find the way for the flowing together to happen and experience the releasing and dynamism that come from that partnership. This kind of dynamism is released when there comes a clearing of the air of the things that surface when we confront ourselves and realize how much we have been shaped by the society rather than by God's Spirit. The church was birthed to become an agency for expressing the divine will of God. This included salvation of human beings through the spread of the gospel, recovery of human boldness with the power of the Spirit, and nurture of human understanding to the truth of God's Word.

QUESTIONS

1. Hayford discloses several occasions in his life when he discovered hidden racism in his heart. Have you had similar experiences when God has convicted you? How has God moved to change you? How have those changes shown in your life?

2. How is God holding your congregation accountable about the matter of racism?

3. If your congregation were to take seriously the call to a multi-ethnic partnership, what first steps would be necessary? Who would need to be involved?

3 | Color Lines and the Religion of Racism

LEONARD LOVETT

THE LATE AFRICAN AMERICAN social historian and warrior for the race W. E. B. DuBois made a prediction and a prophetic indictment of racism in our nation a century ago that has proved to be momentous in our time. DuBois admonished the United States that the greatest problem facing America during the twentieth century would be the problem of the color line.[1] This prophetic pronouncement was made on the eve of the birth of the pentecostal movement at the dawn of the twentieth century during the most racist period in our history. Recently as I stood at the final resting place of DuBois in Accra, Ghana, located in West Africa, I wept as I praised God for the light that passed through this giant of a person for our time and place in history.

"Color line" was the term adopted by DuBois for "racism." Racism at its core is fundamentally a spiritual problem with apparent social manifestations. While prejudice has to do with prejudging or making categorical generalizations about others without having the facts, racism differs. The roots of racism lie deep within the soil of human pride and the pervasive will to be different and superior. Racism presupposes dominance. It has to do with the abuse and misuse of power by the dominant group.

Because racism is grounded in pride (hubris, which is the exaltation of the self), it may very well be classified as one of the sins of the spirit. Racism arrogates unto itself the element of power and utilizes it for the purpose of subjugating those who are different. Apart from the element of power, racism is reduced to bigotry. Power is crucial for the creation, perpetuation, and maintenance of racism within a given society.

If we are to grapple with the problem of racism as it is manifested in North America, we must become intentional about pursuing the challenges that African Americans experience on a day-to-day basis and the residual effects on people of color globally. It may mean leaving our comfort zones and encountering oppressed persons on their level of social existence.

From a theological-ethical perspective, racism is a moral and spiritual problem. It is the perverse worship of the self, rooted in spiritual pride. Racism is self-deification in its purest form. Self-glorification and arrogant ingratitude constitute the essential notion of sin. Racism is much more than ingratitude. It is itself religion. It is a decisive act of turning away from God. It is life according to the flesh (Rom. 8:5). It is the worship of the creature rather than the Creator. God is displaced by human machinations.[2]

MENDING FENCES: CAN'T WE ALL GET ALONG?

Not long ago, Diane Sawyer asked the Rev. Billy Graham on *Prime Time Live* what he would choose if he could wave his hand and make one problem in this world go away. Billy Graham responded, "Racial division and strife." Few issues disturb contemporary society so persistently as the conflict between various ethnic groups. To break down the divisive walls of hostility will require a different kind of solution from any that Congress can provide.

A word from Scripture speaks to our common origins and at the same time challenges our pride, the soil from which our racial division stems. God has made "of one blood all nations" of persons to dwell on the face of the earth (Acts 17:26 KJV). That timeless truth alone is the basis for our common humanity and ground.

Racism in modern times is the consequence of a distorted view of the unity of humankind espoused in Scripture. Such unity makes allowance for uniqueness and diversity. The fact that we are indeed different is the pivotal point that highlights our need to recognize our common humanity at another level of social existence. The perceived tacit assumptions embraced by believers of all races must come under severe scrutiny and judgment if we are to participate with God as a new community comes into being. Is not this an aspect of the beatific vision of John the revelator who saw people from every "ethnos" entering God's dominion?

In God's dominion, the "first shall be last; and the last shall be first" (Matt. 19: 30 KJV). Christ's is the only dominion where the slave becomes the master and the master becomes the slave. We are called and challenged to be the "salt of the earth" in a world that is under the judgment of the Fall. In the midst of a fallen world, the dominion of God has a unique transforming character. Following the mandates of God's dominion, we are compelled to create and maintain a just and humane society. We are not compelled to create a utopian society; we are compelled to be witnesses in the midst of a "crooked world."

Many persons of color are rejecting Eurocentric views of Christianity. With the rise of Afrocentric thought in our time, many African American believers are striving to comprehend the teachings of Scripture in the context of African and African American history and culture. There appears to be widespread rejection of the blond, blue-eyed Europeanized Christ, the product of an artist's imagination. I recall as a lad in Florida our attempt to trust this Christ while at the same time knowing deep within that something was lacking.

In those days the numbers never came out right at the end of the farming year. We were always in debt and not of our own choosing. We learned that we had been victimized by a farming sharecropping system that was set in motion to keep African Americans enslaved for some eight decades beyond emancipation. That was merely good business for entrepreneurs who were supposedly marvelous white Christians on Sunday and oppressors the rest of the week. Such misdeeds became the basis for business as usual. Increasingly frustrated with an unjust racist system, we had no better place to turn than the black church. It had been the vanguard for freedom since its emergence as an "invisible institution" during the antebellum period of our sojourn in this strange land. The African American preacher held high a beacon of hope to our slave forebears whose ancestors had also endured many dark nights of slavery. That is why African Americans are not afraid to sing, in songs such as "How I Got Over," "My soul looks back and wonders how I got over."

Once we discovered the manly Christ of Scripture, we became uncomfortable with a Eurocentric Christ who did not square with our personhood and humanity. We longed for a Christ who could break the bonds of oppression and set the captives free. We longed for a God whose promises were sure, regardless of what it took. We longed for a God who would rend the heavens and come down to participate with a people bound in a covenental relationship. Such thinking forms the basis for our growing impatience with the perceived racism of white Christians.

The "not guilty" verdict in the O. J. Simpson trial brought to the surface private sentiments of our national racial xenophobia. The media did not lure us unto the great divide on race; it merely validated what was seething beneath the surface in blacks and whites alike. I could hardly open my lecture notes on that afternoon at a well-known university. I was pressed in my thoughts about the verdict. After skillfully using the avoidance response, I decided to speak with firm candor. I reminded the young mixed audience that white Americans tasted in one day what African Americans had been enduring for more than four centuries on this continent. Rodney King's question in 1992, "Can we all get along?" merited a response. My pessimistic and resounding no to this question created silence in the room. My pessimism has firm roots and grounding in my Christian optimism. Apart from a radical reorientation, it is impossible for us to get along at this juncture in history. The task of mending fences is both human and divine.

BUILDING BRIDGES: SEARCH FOR COMMON GROUND

Ultimately, our human search for common ground should never end with a naturalism grounded in humanism.[3] At the pinnacle of faith for the disinherited stands Jesus Christ the Great Emancipator who not only symbolizes but also is higher ground. He alone connects us all. The writer of First Peter reminds us that "judgment must begin at the house of God" (4:17 KJV). Why must judgment begin with the community of faith? Because our egotistical pride must come under condemnation. The left hand of God's judgment is poised to strike deep within the community of faith to purge the body of the virulence of racism.

The apostle Paul reminded the Christians at Philippi that "our citizenship is in heaven" (Phil. 3:20 NKJV). We possess dual citizenship. Our earthly walk is here but our hearts are there. Our primary loyalty is rooted in our love and allegiance to the God of another community. The norms we embrace within this earthly community are grounded in our commitment and ultimate allegiance to the God of glory. Our citizenship in that transcendent community is the standard.

Our heavenly citizenship alone is the ultimate measuring rod by which we determine what is in fact right or wrong, just or unjust, good or unrighteous. We do not live by fads or trends, opinion polls or majority vote. Our heavenly citizenship is the acid test by which we critique the behavior of nations as well as persons. Because we are citizens of two worlds, there is a sense in which we live "between the times." Our dual citizenship informs the judgments and norms we render, the conclusions we form. However, we are more than resident aliens in this world. Our task is not to Christianize the political order but to be a witness in the midst of unjust conditions. We live in both the now and the not yet. In the words of Martin Luther King Jr., we "march to the tune of a distant drummer."

Martin Luther King Jr. was God's gift to our times. He was indeed the most vocal social prophet of our generation. I met Martin during my junior year at Morehouse College. In the near reaches of my memory I can hear that baritone voice ringing from the steps of the Atlanta University quadrangle as King admonished us to stand up for what is right and to exercise our constitutional and God-given right to protest injustice in the name of God. King recognized the spiritual dimension of racism and segregation. King combined the nonviolent philosophy of Gandhi with the love ethic of Jesus and formulated a potent strategy against segregation.

A significant point is that the black church was the base from which King waged his militant struggle against the rabid forces of segregation. Martin's dream was the driving force behind his struggle for downtrodden persons. Martin was consistent throughout his lifetime as he passionately challenged the powers that be. On the final evening of his life, King delivered his final message from the historic Mason Temple in Memphis, headquarters of the Church of God in Christ, the oldest and largest primarily African American pentecostal movement in North America.

The Mason Temple was named for the Church of God in Christ founder, the late Bishop Charles Harris Mason, a "spiritual graduate" of the 1906 Azusa Street revival. It was during this revival led by William J. Seymour, according to eyewitness Frank Bartleman, that the color line was "washed away by the blood." The fact that a few years beyond the Azusa revival many ethnics went their own way was proof that the color line was not washed away by the blood. Where the Holy Spirit is regnant and allowed to work, the color line will be "overcome by the blood." We see color, but the power in the blood enables Christians to transcend the vestiges of color and racism and become all we were meant to be for one another with a love that knows no boundaries.

King had the right vision for the United States, but our nation did not heed his admonition. Had the European American church collectively and prophetically indicted racism in word and deed a few decades ago, the problem of the color line would have been virtually resolved. Martin presented the right diagnosis as he dramatized the evils of segregation. He knew that the collective conscience of our nation was not ready to hear a word of judgment. Radical surgery precedes healing; judgment precedes grace; justice precedes love; forgiveness precedes reconciliation; repentance precedes redemption. The church must be committed to the eradication of the core of racism in the United States and to healing the deep wounds it has cut into the fabric of the country's landscape.

Currently, I am not as disturbed by the resurgence of the Ku Klux Klan and militant right-wing groups as I am by the silence of the Christian church. The primary obligation of the church is to set its own house in order. Judgment must begin in the house of God. We are reminded and challenged by Jesus Christ that "every kingdom divided against itself is brought to desolation, and every city or house divided against itself will not stand" (Matt. 12:25 NKJV). This is no less true for the faith community. What can we do now given the urgency of the moment?

ON DOING THE RIGHT THING

"The axe is laid unto the root of the trees" is a word of judgment in Scripture (Matt. 3:10 KJV). Interracial bridges of understanding can be built when white Americans, through genuine repentance, confess their sinfulness, racism, and racial pride. In addition they should in spiritual humility and faith:

- Courageously explode racial myths and seek to cultivate relationships and values around common goals on common ground.
- Build partnerships with ethnic pastors in the inner city by initiating workshops, worship experiences, and other encounters that will foster a deepened understanding of African Americans and other minorities.

- Seek wisdom in underwriting a specific ministry to the inner city through positive love and genuine concern, not personal and collective guilt.

African Americans and other minorities must also bear the burden of praying for those who stand on the other side and view them as being different. This will require a certain amount of courage and resolve. It will require a kind of disciplined "tough love" to come to grips with those who oppress us and find a place to begin. African Americans, too, must come to the table with a real sense of humility:

- Pray that amid inner-city squalor African Americans and other minorities will come to understand that the real enemy is not necessarily "whitey," that another enemy has crept in overnight and perverted our internal value system. It is foolish to waste time striking back at a society perceived to be the enemy.
- Pray especially for African Americans to stop demeaning their personhood by senseless and destructive black-on-black patterns of behavior and to be open to a living experiment with "others" who are different.
- Pray that through education, responsible media, drama, art, and the bold proclamation of the gospel, African Americans and other minorities will be challenged to a love and allegiance for Jesus that will enable them to cease destructive behaviors toward any brother or sister, anyone blessed with the gift of life in the image of our Creator.

Together we must all pray:

- That churches will take the leadership role in encouraging racial unity within diversity. The melting pot conceptual metaphor, which suggests fusion of identity, is no longer relevant. The "salad bowl" concept, which suggests retention of one's ethnic/racial identity within a pluralistic culture, is far more compatible with the goal of liberation.
- That white Americans, African Americans, Latinos, and all minorities must begin to pray, struggle, and genuinely contend for a world in which God's dominion causes us to lay aside our human, racial, ethnic, nationalistic, and warring allegiances. We must pray for a world in which all, living under the mandates of God's dominion, celebrate life, joyfully affirming that Jesus is Sovereign.

At a more pragmatic level we are exhorted by the prophet Micah to "do justice." Praxis must always follow a theoretical conversion. Racism will not vanish after a great dialogue about its presence. We must act with a deep sense of urgency as a community of the concerned. You as an individual can make these efforts:

- Create a personal visionary statement opposing racism. Proceed to develop a global vision to end racism.
- Be courageous to explore other cultures.
- Invite persons of a different ethnic origin to your home.
- Know your community and come to recognize racist behavioral patterns within your community.
- Pray for the courage to uncover, challenge, and expose institutional racism in your community.
- Avoid biased or slanted language about persons who are different.
- Envision a "rainbow-conscious" church embracing all by modeling the ideal of diversity.
- Avoid investing your money in financial institutions that invest their funds in countries with a poor human rights track record.

In discussions about racism learn to focus on issues rather than personalities. Learn to bridge differences rather than insist on similarity of viewpoints:

- Build bridges of mutual understanding and trust rather than second-guess where others are coming from.
- Pray consistently about ending racism as though all depended upon God, and work consistently against racism as though all depended upon you.
- Develop and cultivate the capacity to be proactive rather than reactive in your response to racism.
- Know who you are historically and culturally: identity.
- More significantly, remember whose you are: spiritual identity.

CONCLUSION

Within the household of faith, repentance should precede bridge building and reconciliation. There must be a deep and radical purging of the human spirit before God. We must sound a collective call for massive repentance in the body of Christ. The church is called in strange ways to live upon its knees in open repentance before the Creator. "Woe is me" must always precede "Here am I." The fruits of repentance should be modeled in our Christian conferences and confabs. Christian conferences, both African American and European American, should reflect racial diversity. We must begin to model God's dominion in everything that we do so we can truly be a light to the nations.

The Christian community should insist that our nation make real the promise of democracy by extending equal treatment to all people regardless of ethnic origins who are seeking asylum in our land. Immigration laws have been recently revised to accommodate an influx of persons fleeing conflict in Eastern Europe. The arrival of large numbers of persons seeking political asylum has placed additional strain upon an already struggling economy, thus jeopardizing entry-level jobs for citizens of color. Simultaneously, newly created policies are prohibiting the entrance of Haitians and others from the Southern Hemisphere who seek to enjoy the same privileges extended to Cubans and other persons of a lighter hue. As Christians "living between the times," we must be prepared to challenge these injustices in the name of the God who takes sides with oppressed persons.

Ultimately and finally, we must seek to overcome our tragic divisions both within the community of faith and within the larger society. Jesus Christ is the point of connection. We were created for responsible obedience to God and for genuine community with other persons. Authentic spirituality must undergird our relationship to those who are different. Only then can we begin to view them through the lenses of the One who was the essence of compassion. Unless we have sat where oppressed persons have sat, we are ill prepared to make judgments about the realities they experience on a day-to-day basis.

To take Jesus seriously is to become "offended" by him. The Greek word rendered in the Christian Scriptures is *scandalizo*. It means to stumble or trip over something Jesus has said, to become so disturbed by it that you are actually propelled toward greater faith. It may be that if we are not disturbed by the words of Jesus concerning the presence of racism within the community of faith and the larger society, if we are not scandalized by the words of Jesus concerning a household divided against itself, then perhaps we have never really understood him. As a radically committed Christian, I believe that in history the Lamb will overcome the lion.

QUESTIONS

1.   Lovett makes many suggestions for specific anti-racist actions you or your congregation might undertake. Which of them are you already doing? Which of them might you add to your anti-racist work?

2.   Note the differences between Lovett's suggested prayers for African American and white Christians. What do you learn about the situations of both groups from those differences?

3.   How can the preservation of our cultural variety contribute to the eradication of racism?

4.   What does it mean to be people willing to affirm metanoia and call attention to the reality of racism?

4 | Combating Racism in Church and Seminary

SUSAN E. DAVIES

HOW DOES ONE ADDRESS RACISM in an environment that seems racially and culturally homogeneous? I am an English-speaking white woman living in the northern part of one of the "whitest" states in the United States. Even though I live in the second largest city in the state and nearly eighty languages are spoken in Maine, it is not unusual for me to go weeks meeting only European Americans.

Five hundred African American people live here in Bangor, which has a population of 35,000. One thousand members of the Penobscot Nation live on a reservation nine miles north of the city. The Asian and Middle Eastern communities in this area now number about 350 and 300, respectively. The three synagogues have a combined membership of 1,000, and the one kosher restaurant serves all of northern Maine. The Islamic community, based at the university, has grown to nearly 300 and is building the first mosque in the state. The 200,000-member Franco-American community has three-hundred-year-old roots in Maine and is spread throughout the state. They and the Native American nations are the primary focus of racial and ethnic hostility here.

In a state of 1.2 million people, less than 0.5 percent are African American; self-identified racial/ethnic groups other than Franco-Americans make perhaps an additional 1 percent. My rare encounters with Asian or African American people are examples not only of the "whiteness" of this environment, but also of the segregated nature of this part of the United States and the covert as well as overt racism on which it is built.

Within the last two years, three well-publicized racially motivated incidents have occurred. In each case the media have covered the events as strange exceptions to an otherwise racially untroubled situation. In a small community an hour from here, an eight-year-old girl, afraid of her parents' wrath when she was late from school, claimed that a black man in a red truck had tried to molest her on the way home. The resultant search was called off a day later when the girl acknowledged her lie. Several months ago, a black couple returned to their trailer in an even smaller community to find nothing but ashes. They had been in conflict with the town officers about a restaurant they had purchased. No one has been charged with the arson. Last week a young black man was stabbed on the streets of Bangor by another young man who had just hours before shouted "nigger" and brandished a shotgun at the black man from a passing car.

A second Maine branch of the National Association for the Advancement of Colored People (NAACP) has been reorganized on the campus of the University of Maine, four miles north of Bangor. The Portland branch has worked diligently for years against racism in the schools, in the police forces, and in the public and private sectors. Native Americans, Franco-Americans, increasing numbers of Asian Americans, and African Americans in Maine can all tell painful stories of personal and corporate acts of racially and ethnically based bigotry.

Still, few of the all-white churches with whom I worship on Sunday mornings as a visiting preacher believe they have any pressing reasons for thinking of themselves as racist. Outside of Bangor and Portland, white people are the visual, structural, numerical, and theological norm here. The occasional "Undoing Racism" workshop offered through the Peace and Justice Center is rarely attended by or promoted through church folks. The comfortable assumptions of white supremacy remain unchallenged by daily life and work, and whenever the question is raised, the response is often, "We don't have that problem because none of 'them' live here."

I live and work in a situation where the greatest obvious sources of conflict are the political results of religious difference between white churches, the painful struggles between white people around gender, sexual orientation, abortion rights, and inclusive language for God, and the devastation caused poor rural people of every racial and ethnic background by the massive international economic shifts.

If racism is to be part of the consciousness of white people who live in such places, we must work to make it so. Whiteness as the norm has been so completely built into our thinking patterns and our religious imagery that we notice it as little as a fish sees water. Very little in the media or in the church challenges us to recognize the evil eating at our souls.

The following pages are addressed primarily to white people who live in similar situations of apparent monoculturalism. I have tried to begin at the beginning, inside my life as a white woman, in order to communicate with those who live in similar contexts.

HOW RACISM WORKS IN THE UNITED STATES

Racism is an insidious and deadly structural condition that infects all European American people raised in the United States. It also affects every person who lives in this country. For Christians, racism is a corrosive and deadly sin that subverts and denies God's creation and salvation of the world. We have all been equally formed in the image of God, and we have been equally offered salvation in the life, death, and resurrection of Christ. Support for a system of psychological and social structures that elevate one racial group above another is acquiescence in evil because it denies the good news of God in Jesus Christ. This chapter names some of the ways white racism infects both church and society in the United States and describes one process by which theological education can work to expose and combat the delusive structure.

Most European American church members have great difficulty grasping the depth and complexity of the structural racism that permeates North American institutions. Most white Americans have been raised in a cocoon in which verbal, visual, and social structures have embedded a false knowledge that normative human beings are white and middle class (as well as male, able-bodied, and heterosexual). School and church school texts published by white denominations until the last fifteen years were illustrated with white children who had occasional friends not fitting that norm. Until the 1960s, white-owned mass-distribution newspapers and newsmagazines regularly described the ethnicity or race of anyone who was not northern European or perceived as "white," but omitted the racial descriptor for Anglo-Americans. Television and films from their origin until the 1970s depicted Native Americans as bloodthirsty savages or pathetic victims, Asian Americans as opium-smoking men and sexually exotic women, Latin Americans as wetbacks or members of street gangs, and African Americans as wide-eyed fools, menacing dangers, dancing wonders, or super-human athletes. (If you doubt these depictions, watch a few old movies on cable for a refresher course.) White middle-strata churches have been and remain the most segregated sectors of our society, more so than workplaces or schools.

I am a white Anglo-Saxon Protestant woman whose work on unpacking North American racism began in my teens and still continues. I proceed in fits and starts, sometimes carefully unpacking the layers of normative and structural racism in which I have been formed, and sometimes suddenly confronting both my fears and my actions.

During the summer of 1994 I was faced once again with how deeply racism is embedded in my psyche as well as in our social structures. I was traveling through airports while the preliminary hearings in the O. J. Simpson case were being broadcast. Many people were watching in Indianapolis and Newark. On the plane between airports I read several newspaper articles on the perceptual differences between the black and white communities regarding both police procedures and the probability of Mr. Simpson's guilt or innocence. When I arrived in Newark, I saw at least five well-dressed couples in which the man was black and the woman was white. As I passed them in the walkways, images of knives and blood rose before my eyes, and I found myself concerned about the safety of those women.

Within living memory in the United States, a black man who even looked a white woman in the eye was liable to lynching. Forty years ago, white girls were warned about the sexual prowess and potential violence of black men. Movies, comic books, newspaper articles, and table conversation even in the "unprejudiced" North were filled with warnings about dangers posed for innocent and virtuous white girls around dangerous and unstable black men. Suddenly all that long-forgotten material came rushing back, and I was faced once again with the insidious nature of structural and psychological racism. Retired Detective Mark Furman's vicious and rabid racism is only a more apparent version of what lurks in even the most genteel white Americans.

Racism blurs all white Americans' vision as much as the wrong lenses in our glasses blur our sight. The process of eradicating it is difficult, slow, and often painful. It is also a requirement of God's justice.

Racism as a Social Structure

Racism is a socially constructed relationship between groups within any given society. The dominant cultural, political, and economic group defines one or more other groups as inherently of lesser human value based on the others' racial or ethnic origin and enforces that definition with its social, political, and economic power.

White racism is present in both the inner lives and the social realities of European Americans. As another white educator, Peggy McIntosh, has encouraged us, we need to look at particularities of how racism is present in everyday transactions.[1] In my case, racism meant that when I left my check-cashing card and license home last year, I was fairly sure the supermarket manager would let me cash a check without having my appearance work against me. It meant that when a white friend's white son was harassed by high school bullies, I did not wonder how much of the beating was the result of his race. But when a white friend's black son was similarly harassed, I did wonder.

Racism means that when I look in the mirror I see "only" a woman, not a "white" woman. It means that when I turn on the television, I see people like me represented in all of the ads, in almost every news story, and in almost every situation comedy. It means, in Peggy McIntosh's words, that "I can criticize our government and talk about how much I fear its policies and behaviors without being seen as a cultural outsider."[2] It means that I can buy nylon stockings and Band-Aids and blemish covers in "flesh" tones that "match" my skin. It means that I can see advertisements for hair care products that suit my needs on English-language broadcasts. It means that I can use church school materials without worrying whether my friend's daughter will see herself in the pictures. It means, again in McIntosh's words, that "I can take a job with an affirmative action employer without having co-workers on the job suspect that I got it because of race."[3]

Racism as a Sinful Social Reality

These examples have one common thread: they are all based on structures that delude European Americans into thinking we are the norm. The problem with the Band-Aids is not that they are designed to match our skin. The problem is that the label "flesh tone" deludes us into thinking that materials that match our skin are the norm. Sin functions here when we are deluded into making an idol of our condition, our situation, our skin color. I and persons like me become the standard by which other human beings are assessed.

Similarly, affirmative action programs and their backlash, cries of "reverse discrimination," grow out of a delusion of normativity for white people. The structural assumption has been that white people get jobs or promotions because they have worked for them and deserve them. Sometimes that is true; but sometimes white people get the job because they are white. The problem is the assumption that a white skin is more likely to accompany competence than a skin of any other hue.

Seeing oneself on TV—in ads, in shows, on the news—is not problematic. The structural racism appears when some kinds of people see themselves often and in significant positive roles while other kinds of people see themselves seldom and then largely in negative roles, whether as victims, perpetrators, or stereotypes. Those who see themselves often or positively are led into the delusion that they are the norm. They/we then act out of that delusion, distorting relationships and the ability to think about relationships. The distortions are transmitted structurally, and all of us who live in the United States pay a price for the distortions.

COMBATING RACISM IN AN EDUCATIONAL CONTEXT

I teach in a seminary affiliated with the United Church of Christ and have curriculum responsibility in the areas of education and pastoral care. One way to combat racism is to raise consciousness and develop alternative action strategies in the areas for which we have responsibility, whether within the educational systems or in other spaces such as work, political, and personal lives. For the last three years I have been teaching an introductory course in education designed to foster critical thinking about the social construction of reality in society and the church. Although the course is not directly addressed to white racism, racist assumptions and constructions are among those challenged by our study/action.

Work by students has three major components: (1) understanding the social construction of reality, including the analysis of a personal breakthrough experience; (2) an educational biography and accompanying project; and (3) a class teaching session.

The First Component

The first component begins with some of Stephen Brookfield's assumption analysis exercises.[4] Individual and shared assumptions about everyday realities are examined in small groups and class discussions. Assumptions about class, race, and gender, about religion and politics and money, about appropriate roles for men and women, children and older people, are all laid on the table and pulled apart. Racism, in this context, is seen as one of the significant social constructions by which human beings create and sustain their worlds.

Following this work, we move on to William B. Kennedy's structured ideological analysis of breakthrough experiences.[5] The process asks participants to name an occasion in their lives when they could see through the ideological cocoons in which they had been raised. Participants are asked to identify the social influences (family, church, work, school, gender, ethnic or racial identity, media, global events, peers) that encouraged or discouraged their breakthrough into a different way of perceiving themselves in the world. My classroom examples include occasions when I "saw" more clearly the nature of my white racist behaviors and privileges.

Students make their analyses independently and then discuss them in small groups, following which they write a reflection paper on the experience. Of the eighty-three students who have taken the course in the last three years, almost one-third have identified encounters with racist social structures as their breakthrough experiences. Others have seen more clearly the social construction of classism and the ways in which they occupied multiple and conflicting social locations based on their gender, age, race, class, and perceived physical/mental ability.

The final movement in this first section of the course is the reading of Berger and Luckman's *The Social Construction of Reality.*[6] In this work from the 1960s, the authors describe the ways linguistic communities both create and are created by human society. Students respond positively to the opportunity to view white North American culture and church cultures from a critically analytic sociological perspective. For many, the altered angle of vision unlocks new ways of seeing themselves and their social roles.

An example of this opportunity for new vision can be found in one class session years ago. That course section included a Protestant Guatemalan woman who lived with her family in Providence, Rhode Island. Her difficulty in selecting a particular breakthrough experience after years of living in a police state led me to ask her to speak to the class. I invited three other class members to join her: a European American woman who had been an American Baptist missionary to Nicaragua for twelve years, an East German woman who was completing her seminary education at Bangor, and a woman who had always identified herself as white and was raised in a German Lutheran orphanage in Pennsylvania during the depression. Each was asked to speak about the social construction of reality in her particular context.

The missionary discovered that she had to reconstruct completely her religious, social, and political identity as a North American woman in the face of her experiences in Nicaragua during the Contra War against the Sandinista government. She retained her evangelical faith, but now both challenged and rejected most of the political and social structures she had been taught as a child in North American schools and churches. The Guatemalan woman spoke of the power of fear and silence in a country ruled by a particularly brutal military while holding her hands over her ears. The East German woman made connections between the ideological indoctrination of her education with that of American schooling. And the older "white" woman spoke for the first time in sixty-five years of her Hopi father and her loss of identity as a child. By the end of the evening we had (re)discovered the nature of oppressions and the power of reclaiming identity through story. We had also made connections between North American racism and the life experience of individuals and communities.

The Second Component

The second major component of the course is the telling of individual educational biographies in the same small groups. After the biographies are completed, individuals read Thomas Groome's *Christian Religious Education,*[7] interview two other people, and complete a reflection project that is developed at the confluence of three ways of learning: (*a*) reflecting on personal life experience, (*b*) reading from a written text, and (*c*) encountering the life experience of others. Once again, students are encouraged to examine the ways in which competing and conflicting social structures have shaped their lives and the lives of other members of church and society, and to examine the roles of race, class, and gender in that formation.

The Third Component

The third major course component is the selection of a written text from a variety of materials suggested by me or provided by the student to present to the class. Presentations have included art psychotherapy with adult mentally retarded people; analysis of cartoons in church publications for their political content; Spanish poetry, song, and drama as a means of discovering other social realities for white North Americans; a worship service in sign language as a way for hearing people to experience social exclusion; and a card game that dealt privileged and oppressed statuses to individual class members.

Some Results of the Course

Although the course was not designed to address only white racism, readings and examples have intentionally included materials from black churches, the spiritual perspectives and social/political experiences of Native Americans, the particular perspectives of white women in theological education, and the theological work of Asian and Hispanic women. As a result, three women have begun to identify their native heritage in a positive way for the first time, including the Guatemalan woman who had previously identified herself as Spanish; one white working-class man has begun to see his life as a YMCA administrator as an example of the workings of classism; many men and women have gained new language with which to identify their own history as it intersects with broader social movements; and almost all the white class members have achieved a new ability to identify instances of white privilege and structural racism. A further result of the course has been increased participation by students in a variety of social justice ministries.

In each case of new insight, the mechanism seems to have been the combination of (*a*) the tools of structural analysis, (*b*) a mechanism for insight into personal history, (*c*) the opportunity to tell one's own story and receive supportively critical feedback from one's peers, and (*d*) new information that intentionally includes the perspectives of people of different racial, ethnic, and social backgrounds.

CONCLUSION

This work of educating for leadership in the life of the church in the twenty-first century in a predominantly European American setting offers one model for integrating anti-racist work into Christian/theological education in any of its forms. The subject of the course is not North American racism. However, because white racism infects all parts of our society, every course opens itself to the inclusion of anti-racist work. Conscious choice of reading material from a variety of perspectives as well as the inclusion of speakers and other resources that offer a wide range of socioeconomic, gender, and racial perspectives not only enriches the experience for all members of a learning group. Such purposive inclusion also challenges racism by permitting all of us to see ourselves in the subject matter, thereby undercutting the assumption of white normativity.

Each of us is called to seek God's justice in the community and in the workplace. Failure to do so increases both our complicity and our culpability. When white people do nothing to combat the racist assumptions and privileges with which we have been taught to function, we continue to foster the oppressive structures from which we unwittingly benefit. When we fail to act, we acquiesce in the corrosive and deadly sin that subverts and denies God's creation and salvation of the world. However, when we act toward God's justice, we move forward on the journey of joy, which is God's will for all the earth.

QUESTIONS

1. How have your understandings of race and racism changed over your lifetime? How have those changes altered your behavior? What influence has the racial/ethnic population of your region had on those changes?

2. If you are a European American, can you name some instances of white privilege in your life? Is your congregation part of the norm for your community? If it is not, how does it differ from the larger context in which you live? Can or should that difference be valued?

3. In what ways can your religious education program work to combat racism? What adult studies programs might you develop with other congregations?

PART 2

Being the Body of Christ

5 | CASE STUDY:
The Interfaith Conference of Greater Milwaukee's Beyond Racism Project

CHARLOTTE HOLLOMAN AND JACK MURTAUGH

THE INTERFAITH CONFERENCE of Greater Milwaukee is the agency through which eleven denominations collaborate to address the social issues affecting the quality of life in the Greater Milwaukee area. The conference enables the religious community to work together in upholding "the dignity of every person and the solidarity of the human community." Throughout its twenty-five-year history, the Interfaith Conference has addressed such issues as hunger, homelessness, public education, jobs, health care, community development, the environment, alcohol and drugs, and our growing aging population.

CONTEXT

Another area that the Interfaith Conference has sought to address is that of racism in our diverse society. The United States is becoming increasingly multicultural, multiracial, and multilingual. Nowhere is this diversity more apparent than in the metropolitan areas of our country. As in the past, newer immigrants and persons migrating from the rural areas of this country settle in the larger metropolitan areas where they believe jobs may be more plentiful, where public support systems may be more accommodating, and where others who share their cultural, ethnic, or racial identity may already reside. One of the results of this immigration and migration is the concentration of persons of color (any people who have other than "white" European ancestry, including Africans, Asians/Pacific Islanders, Latina/Latinos, Middle Eastern people, Native Americans, and people of "mixed" ancestry, i.e., combinations of ancestries) in the central cities of this country.

The Greater Milwaukee community reflects this national phenomenon. Indeed, the 1990 Census reveals the following:

- 74.9 percent of the residents in Milwaukee County are white (European Americans), and 55 percent of these individuals live in the city of Milwaukee.

[43]

- 20.4 percent of the residents of the county are African American, and 98 percent of these individuals live in the city of Milwaukee.
- 4.7 percent of the residents of the county are designated Hispanic, and 88 percent of these individuals live in the city of Milwaukee. (Note: "Hispanic" is not a racial category; some of the white, African American, and other categories are also Hispanic.)
- 0.7 percent of the residents of the county are Native American, and 84 percent of these individuals live in the city of Milwaukee.
- 1.6 percent of the residents of the county are Asian, and 77 percent of these individuals live in the city of Milwaukee.
- 2.4 percent of the residents of the county are described as "other," and 94 percent of these individuals live in the city of Milwaukee.

Not only do most of the county's persons of color live in the city of Milwaukee, but they also live in highly segregated neighborhoods. A study published by the University of Chicago identified Milwaukee as one of five cities in the nation whose patterns of racial segregation are so clearly drawn that they are deemed "hypersegregated." For the most part, people of color and European Americans live in identifiably separate neighborhoods in this community with few natural opportunities for interacting and for developing personal relationships.

THE BEYOND RACISM PROJECT

In 1989, in response to increasing community concerns about racial tensions in Milwaukee's congregations, businesses, schools, and neighborhoods, the Interfaith Conference convened a Task Force on Racism. They explored ways to address the personal, cultural, and institutional aspects of prejudice and to build support for social change in this area. The work of the task force resulted in the Beyond Racism Project. (Although many names were considered, including Eliminating Racism, the group felt our energy would be better served moving "beyond" or outside the scope of racism.)

The Beyond Racism Project is an ongoing effort to bridge the gap between people of different races and cultures. The mission of the Beyond Racism Project is twofold: to facilitate individual, group, and institutional recognition of and appreciation for our diverse society; and to invite participants to take an active role in addressing the issues of prejudice and racism.

Several programs have been developed to accommodate the diverse needs of groups that wish to use the Beyond Racism Project: Multicultural Dialogues, Dialogues Among People of Color, Building Community, and Alike and Different, a summer program for children.

Multicultural Dialogues

In three sessions of at least two hours each, participants explore the issues of prejudice and racism as they affect individuals and the community. These sessions raise the consciousness of participants and elicit their commitment to confronting these problems through continued education, training, and action. Multicultural Dialogues have been sponsored by the following groups:

CONGREGATIONS

A number of congregations (city and suburban) have sponsored Multicultural Dialogues. When congregations are primarily European American, persons of color who have participated in the Beyond Racism Project are recruited to join in the dialogue. The outcome from this dialogue leads some people to participate in other Beyond Racism programs.

MINISTERIAL ASSOCIATIONS

A ministerial association in a city outside Milwaukee County is implementing the Multicultural Dialogue component in anticipation of a number of persons of color moving into their community. A series of dialogues is taking place.

NEIGHBORHOOD GROUPS

Community-based organizations are sponsoring Multicultural Dialogues for their staff so that they may better serve their targeted multiracial population.

DENOMINATIONAL STAFF

Both local and national staff of denominations are participating in Multicultural Dialogues with sessions longer than just two hours at a time. Plans include the continued use of the Beyond Racism resources. The Lutheran Human Relations Association and Beyond Racism are collaborating in this effort.

STAFF DEVELOPMENT DAYS

Suburban school districts are using the resources of the Beyond Racism Project.

Dialogues among People of Color

These dialogues are facilitated by people of color, and all participants are people of color. Participants share and explore their personal experiences with racism and the impact it has had on their lives. This program includes three sessions of at least two hours each. One primary focus of these sessions is to explore the effects of internalized oppression on people of color.

This component is a difficult program to implement because of the nature of the deep hurts caused by racism. For people of color who have participated, it has been a liberating experience. This component is currently being targeted to service organizations composed of persons of color.

Building Community

The Building Community component requires the participation of equal numbers of European Americans and people of color in each session. This component includes four parts:

1. An introductory overnight retreat that focuses on sharing personal experiences with stories about prejudice and racism.
2. Three six-hour educational sessions focusing on societal racism and on developing the skills for analyzing institutional racism.
3. Four to six meetings of Community Building Groups established across racial/cultural lines.
4. A closing overnight retreat that focuses on planning for future action and on the group's individual and mutual commitment to combating prejudice and racism.

The Building Community component is adaptable to meet a variety of situations. It can be targeted to the needs of adults, young people, and children. Examples include the following:

- The faculty of a local high school committed themselves to a yearlong in-service training related to cultural pluralism and racism. Crossroads Ministry and the Beyond Racism Project collaborated in providing staff and resources for this in-service training.
- A neighborhood organization sponsored the Beyond Racism: Building Community Program for their multiracial neighborhood. They implemented all four parts of the program including overnight retreats.
- A local university committed the faculty of several departments along with students to participate in the Beyond Racism Project from September 1995 to March 1996. They implemented all parts of the Building Community component including overnight retreats.
- A Roman Catholic religious order for women sponsored the Building Community component for members. The order implemented it over a period of one month including a closing retreat.
- Four countywide Beyond Racism: Building Community Programs have

been implemented. Each was conducted over a two-month period that included all four parts of the Building Community Program. A key aspect was the participation of equal members of European Americans and people of color in each session.

Alike and Different

Alike and Different is an antibias, multicultural program that enables children ages four to twelve to explore comfortably the differences and similarities that make up our individual and group identities. The program also helps children develop the skills necessary to identify and counter the hurtful impact of bias against themselves and their peers. Children from all the racial/cultural groups that make up Milwaukee's diverse population participate in this twenty-hour, five-day program.

Alike and Different is being implemented in several ways:

1. For two weeks during the summer children ages four to twelve participated in the Alike and Different Program. They were held at two different locations for one week each. Each day a different racial group was highlighted. Evaluations recommend that Alike and Different Programs for children be held over a two-week period in the same location with the same program.
2. Plans are under way for the Alike and Different curriculum to be included in the summer programs of youth-serving agencies in Milwaukee.
3. Efforts are being made to include Alike and Different Programs in the city and suburban schools during the school year.

CONCLUSION

These models have been and will continue to be adapted to meet the needs of various target audiences. The Beyond Racism: Building Community Program for young people, for instance, has been modified each time it has been presented to accommodate various time and place restraints.

Our experience has reinforced our perception that a nonconfrontational approach is most helpful in engaging people in the process. People are willing to participate actively in the struggle toward new learning when they are not threatened in the process or made to feel guilty. The emphasis on awareness and personal healing has helped people move toward new levels of responsibility in confronting racism.

Relationship building has been a key element of this model. We have found that participants have grown in their understanding of the costs of racism through their informal interaction and their sharing of time and conversation in unstructured settings of their choosing. They have been able to enter one another's worlds and have, therefore, seen the realities and effects of racism in new ways.

Ongoing commitment to long-term change takes place when the participants in a specific program of the Beyond Racism Project are from the same environment or institution. They identify issues that need to be addressed within their neighborhood, school, agency, business, or congregation. The process focuses their attention on these issues, and follow-through steps can be planned. When the participants have no ties to a specific environment or institution, it is more difficult to build a cohesive base for action, to develop their understanding of racism, and to apply their experiences to their own solution. Some participants have arranged for the Beyond Racism Project to be implemented within their environments or institutions. The Beyond Racism Project needs additional resources to build an active and connected base for these participants.

A central principle of the full Beyond Racism model has been to involve equal numbers of persons of color and persons of European heritage. When we have occasionally deviated from the principle, we have consistently found that the process is enhanced and enriched when an equal balance is present within the group. Recruitment within communities of color is extremely important. We have found more persons of European heritage willing to participate. In beginning this work it is crucial to be certain that persons of color are actively engaged in the initial planning stages as well as with the issue of internalized oppression. Dialogues around issues of internalized oppression and some beginning work of healing within communities of color are critical in preparing people to feel safe and ready to participate in the process. Persons of color must also be willing to participate in the Multicultural Dialogues to ensure that their voices are heard within European American communities.

We have found that it is not possible to shortcut the process. The dialogues are essential tools for beginning the process and engaging people's interest in participating at a deeper level.

The model is not a one-time or short-term experience because racism is not one time or short term. Racism is a life event and takes a lifetime commitment to work to dismantle it.

The Beyond Racism Project: Building Community has received several awards. From Project Equality of Wisconsin it received the 1993 Community Service Award, and from Milwaukee Associates in Urban Development (MAUD) it received the 1993 Community Service Achievement Award. In 1993 it received one of four awards given by the National Council of the Churches of Christ in the USA for its effective contributions to bridging the gap between people of different races and cultures. In May 1995 it received the 1995 Racial Justice Award from the YWCA of Greater Milwaukee.

QUESTIONS

1.   What are the differences and similarities between your community and Greater Milwaukee with regard to racial, ethnic, and linguistic complexity? What resources are available to gather information regarding the composition of your community? What might you do with that information to help your religious community address issues of racism?

2.   Which of the four models developed in this case study might be adaptable to your situation? How would you need to change the model to fit your situation?

3.   What steps might your church or religious community take to develop your methods to address racial separation, racist attitudes, and racist structures?

6 | Questions of Inclusion in the Christian Scriptures

ARTHUR FREEMAN

THE CHURCH MUST RECAPTURE the vision of racial inclusivity that is inherent in Christianity and for a while flourished in the civil rights movement in the United States. To recapture the vision, one must critically rethink the tradition, looking at elements in the Judeo-Christian tradition that both do and do not support inclusivity. Ultimately, this is not just a question of rethinking the past but of responding to God's leading within the context of a society divided on many levels.

The current social and economic context of the United States has altered both the forms and the practices of racism within our society. Our times require a new perspective from which to view our situation, one that recognizes racism as an illness affecting us all, albeit in different ways. Peter Paris indicates,

> The face of contemporary racism is mirrored in the fact that white America can flourish without blacks. This is the first time in the nation's history in which such a claim has been plausible.... Blacks are dispensable today in ways that they were not even one generation ago. The principal causes of this recent discovery are twofold: first, the post-industrial structural changes in our economy caused by the technological revolution in communications; and second, the rapid growth of a new immigrant class eagerly absorbing domestic and other unskilled jobs previously held by blacks.[1]

The disenfranchisement of many by the technological revolution, the relocation or decline of heavy industry, and the influx of immigrants as a source of cheap labor affect not only blacks but others as well, including poor whites and white people dependent on blue-collar work. Self-interest often motivates, and European Americans need to recognize that we also have much at stake in our changing society.

In this context, it is essential that the church reclaim a vision of unity in Christ that builds personal relationships across racial barriers and rediscovers a gospel that is not only strong enough to save but is also strong enough to reconcile.[2] This chapter looks to the resources of the Christian Scriptures for a vision of reconciliation and inclusion, drawing particularly upon First Peter. I am specifically looking for principles for including all people within the beloved community.

FINDING THE WORD OF GOD
IN THE WORD OF GOD

The Bible contains within itself a variety of traditions and approaches to inclusion. Thus, to find the word of God on this question within the Word of God is no simple matter. The traditions are partially adaptations of perspectives of the religious cultures within which Judaism and Christianity developed, and partially responses to historic experience and needs. However, within a religious community rules for inclusion or exclusion are seen not as historically conditioned but as eternal and transcendent values. Religious beliefs about inclusion, based on what are understood to be eternal and transcendent values, can provide strong sanction for the inclusion of those whom societal values might exclude.

We need to look to the biblical material not only for answers, but also for an understanding of the struggles of the early church with the questions. In viewing its struggle we may find a variety of answers and insights into the issues. Thus, we are informed—but not by a simple, singular answer.

Whenever I argue that biblical materials not only provide meaningful answers and a word of God to us, but also in some ways can be harmful; whenever I argue that the early church was on the way to finding answers, sometimes following blind alleys rather than offering an eternal answer to every contemporary question; whenever I argue that the living God does not abdicate God's active role to Scripture written long ago in a different culture; whenever I make these arguments, the conservative and evangelical part of me feels uncomfortable, as though I had betrayed someone or something. As a bishop of my church, I must also be sensitive to the faith others hold that is very similar to the position from which I began my journey in faith. And yet I believe that Jesus himself used a critical methodology with regard to his Scriptures, the Hebrew Scriptures, which was theological-critical in nature, not historical-critical. God's call to justice and Jesus' practice ask that we explore critically how our biblical interpretations can foster—and often have fostered—perspectives that are harmful to others.

A Biblical Paradigm: First Peter

First Peter presents a model from which to approach inclusion. It was written to help the Christian churches in Asia Minor work out their identity in the face of a society that did not hold their values. If the apostle Peter is behind it, as I understand him to be, it represents a tremendous personal transformation of one who resisted dealing with the same issues at his confession of Jesus.[3]

The prescript to the letter reminds the Christians of Asia Minor of their identity. The Greek text is clearer as to the intent of the author than most of the English translations. The letter is addressed to the "elect exiles of the Dispersion." Usually, "elect" and "exiles" are separated in the translation, but they are intentionally together in the Greek to indicate that what elects one also exiles one. For the sake of simplicity I will leave out the Roman provinces mentioned in the address to the churches so that it is clear how the following prepositional phrases qualify "elect exiles":

> Peter, an apostle of Jesus Christ,
> to the elect exiles of the Dispersion [of the listed provinces]
>> according to the foreknowledge of God the Father
>> by the sanctification of the Spirit
>> for obedience to and the sprinkling of the blood of Jesus Christ

To understand the language, it is important to recognize that behind the last prepositional phrase stands the covenant ceremony of Exodus 24: the pledge of obedience and sprinkling with blood. Each prepositional phrase qualifies "elect exiles." One becomes an "elect exile" by the knowledge and intent of God the Father, by the setting apart action of the Holy Spirit, and the purpose of this is obedience to Christ and the establishment of the covenant bond in Christ's blood. The same action of God that elects one also makes one an exile within his or her world. The letter is clear that one derives one's values from God, not the world.

That the Christian is exiled within his or her world is further made clear by the opening prayer (1:3–5 RSV):

> Blessed be the God and Father of our Lord Jesus Christ! By his great mercy we have been born anew to a living hope through the resurrection of Jesus Christ from the dead, and to an inheritance which is imperishable, undefiled, and unfading, kept in heaven for you, who by God's power are guarded through faith for a salvation ready to be revealed in the last time.

Christians' Primary World

Peter calls us to awareness of our primary world, which is God's, and to a critical appraisal of our secondary world, which has ways of ordering life that may not reflect God's values and may be used by evil. The same act of God that elects us to God's world exiles us within our historical-cultural context. Those who are included within God's world, and therefore the Christian community, are those whom God has set apart. God's action is the basis for inclusion into the church and separation from the world.

Yet those so included, exiled from their secondary world, cannot reject their responsibility for this secondary world. The household code in 1 Peter 2:11–17 is the only one in the Christian Scriptures that is primarily focused on the relationship of the Christian to the non-Christian world. The gist of this code is that the church must live redemptively for the world as did Christ, so that the world might be brought to God (see particularly 3:18). This meant much more than the evangelism of the world. To bring the world to God involved the living of God's life in relationship to others and drawing them into this life. Above all it meant to "honor" or respect all humanity (2:17): "Honor all, love the community in which we are brothers and sisters, reverence God, honor the emperor."[4] Thus, Christian freedom from the world is a freedom for the world.

Inclusion and Exclusion within the Christian Community

First Peter provides a striking model in which God-given identity calls the Christian to the inclusion into community of those similarly called and to the inclusion of the world and all humankind within God's redemptive concern. Though God is portrayed here as inclusive, there are other standards within the Jewish and Christian tradition, such as righteousness and holiness, that are in paradoxical tension with this portrayal of God's desire to include. These standards at times are debated within the tradition, and Jesus himself seems to have challenged some of them.[5] However the church understands standards of inclusion and exclusion, the church must consider at least two things. First, the gospel is for all, and its embodiment in baptism is for all who would receive it. Thus, in Christ all other distinctions pass away or are minimized (Gal. 3:27). The standards of inclusion-exclusion can be considered only after one has remembered that God's grace has been given prior to the raising of issues related to the standards. Second, one must look for the direct action of God in persons' lives where God's involvement would seem to indicate some type of inclusion, even if it presents a challenge to the standards that limit inclusion.

Righteousness and Holiness

Righteousness and holiness are biblical standards often used to determine inclusion or exclusion. When a Christian community takes seriously the parts of the Bible that advocate righteousness and holiness as standards, that community is allowing the standards to determine its willingness to embrace or exclude.

In the Bible, righteousness has to do with behavior: it is the life and conduct that God requires of persons who are in covenant. Paul, in Romans 1–3 and Galatians 3, indicates that human beings cannot meet God's conditions for righteousness, and so God declares one's righteousness as a generous gift, though in some Christian Scriptures' traditions this is not well understood or valued.[6] Holiness, on the other hand, is an attribute of God and is the character and nature of what belongs to God. Holiness makes something essentially different. It has a power and glory affecting whatever it touches and can be disturbed by the profane and common.

The primary discussion of holiness in the Hebrew Scriptures is in the priestly book of Leviticus. Israel is called upon to "distinguish between the holy and the common, and between the unclean and the clean" (10:10 RSV). To be holy as God is holy (11:44–45) is then to allow oneself to become a part of the reality that is God's, to belong to God's sphere of existence, and to separate oneself from every possible contaminant to this holiness. Anyone who profanes a holy thing of God should be cut off from God's people (19:8). Too intimate a contact with God's holiness is overwhelming and could produce death (16:2).

In the Christian Scriptures the theme of holiness as the character of God's people is picked up primarily in First Peter where the theme of Leviticus is quoted: "As obedient children, do not be conformed to the passions of your former ignorance, but as he who called you is holy, be holy yourselves in all your conduct; since it is written, 'You shall be holy, for I am holy'" (1:14–16 RSV).

In First Peter the emphasis is primarily ethical, but there are other implications, such as the separation of the Christian from the society as an exile. For Peter this holiness also means that one must be for one's world because this is the character of God's holiness. Thus, holiness does not have to be protected from foreign contaminants or from persons who by their previous lives could be regarded as unclean, nor does holiness need to separate one from others in the world.

First Peter and 1 Corinthians 7:14 indicate that holiness may be regarded as more than a "state of being" to be protected from others. Rather, it becomes active: God's turning toward the world and reaching out toward what is not yet holy but needs to be hallowed. Martin Buber and Franz Rosenzweig, in their famous translation of the Hebrew Scriptures from Hebrew into German that sought to preserve the idiom of the Hebrew, used "hallowing" instead of "holy" to translate the active implications of the Hebrew *kadosh*.[7]

"Holiness" indicates a state that separates the one who is holy from others who are not (as indicated in the Levitical approach) while "hallowing" indicates a transformative outreach toward the world that does not separate the world into sacred and profane. Although all to which holiness reaches out needs transformation, true holiness reaches out rather than withdraws.

PARALLELS TO RACISM

The parallel to the issues in racism is the question of whether one can incorporate into relationship a person who is regarded as different not only because of tradition, culture, and behavior (the person's right[eous]ness or unright[eous]-ness), but also because of the person's being or essence (holiness or nonholiness). Racial distinctions often imply difference in being, in the acceptability of one's person. Each racial group may regard its biological form, traditions, and culture (its way of being) as constituting the identity that makes one really human and of ultimate value. We sanctify our way of being by claiming for it divine or religious sanction. Thus, we give blessing to our separation from others for whatever reason (fear, economics, gender, race). By this we protect our way of being from challenge by the differences of others. Moreover, because we view our way of being as holy or incorporated into God's way of being, we grant ourselves not just identity in God, but identity over against others whose being is not so incorporated and blessed.

A New Perspective

Biblical concerns for both righteousness and holiness must be seen in terms of the perspectives they encourage and the ways in which they legitimize separation from others. According to Acts 10, it took a vision from God to convince Peter that "what God has cleansed, you must not call common." And that had to happen three times before Peter was finally convinced (Acts 10:15–16 RSV). Peter never seemed to find it easy to change his perspective. Both the action of God portrayed in Acts (on behalf of the inclusion of the Gentiles) and First Peter's emphasis on God's holiness (indicating not only separation from the world's values but God's being for the world) call upon Christians to interpret holiness and righteousness as moving them toward the world rather than away from it. God is the God for whom no supposed ontological otherness can create separation from others or diminish their dignity. Then if God is for the world, is God not also in this world? And if God is in this world, is it not also in some sense holy?

The Boundaries Are God's

To whatever extent we feel others may not fit our standards of righteousness or holiness, to whatever extent we are uncomfortable with others' differences, we ultimately must raise the question of who sets the boundaries for inclusion. Although we may very well admit that in the final analysis God sets the boundaries, often we mean God's boundaries as understood within the Bible or within the established traditions of the church. We are not willing to see as the determinant God's contemporary action by which God now accepts and includes.

Much of the literature in the Christian Scriptures is uncomfortably clear that God continues and will continue to play a significant role in the ongoing life of the church. God has not simply turned the church over to its human leadership. Persons responsible for the ongoing life of the church and the preservation of its institutional and spiritual life certainly must deal with boundaries, but we must always ask how our boundaries relate to God's boundaries. How will we come to terms with those whom we exclude but God would include?

The biblical assumption is that God's action and gift of relationship are foundational to the process that constitutes the church. The constitution of the church was never delegated to the church itself, for God no more took a rest after God's saving action in Jesus than after God's creative action in Genesis (John 5:17). The action by which God in the Spirit (described in Acts 1–15) included the Gentiles in a church that had been largely Jewish continuously drove the church beyond its boundaries. God's words to Peter in his vision are profound in their implications: "What God has cleansed, you must not call common" (Acts 10: 15 RSV).

AN INCLUSIVE VISION OF THE CHURCH

If inclusivity is to be determined primarily by the action of God, then the person in whose life God works and whom God calls to Christian community must be included in some way. Personal differences, racial differences, sexual differences, differences of intellectual capacity, differences of moral development or spirituality may not be allowed to exclude those whom God seems to include. In Christ there is no Jew or Greek, slave or free, male or female, African American, European American, Asian American, or Native American, but all are God's children.

Ultimately, only God can determine inclusion. The inclusive church can provide a welcome place for those who are on a spiritual journey and whom God is drawing to God's self. Thus, its ability to do evangelism is enhanced. The inclusive church can call upon the creativity and devotion of persons with varied gifts and of varied backgrounds and races. Thus, its inner life and ministry are enhanced. The inclusive church will seek to provide the life, love, and fellowship that God offers to humanity. Thus, it can be the place of God, the body of Christ, and the hesitating start toward a new humanity. In such a church there will be conflict, but the conflict that is part of relationship and difference, not the conflict that by its very nature seeks to divide, exclude, and destroy. In such a church there will be human imperfection, but also persons who are struggling with growth and responsibility. In such a church variety will feel at home, as will the sacred obligation to live with difference and with love and with God. Such a church cannot be a "homogeneous unit," a community of the like and similar. Any human community could be that. God's community is more. The Pentecost experience called together "devout men from every nation under heaven" (Acts 2:5 RSV).

With those inside the church Christians will usually sense the sharing of something common despite differences, but in the case of those outside the church the other is more fully other and often seems "strange." And yet God calls us to be for this world, and if God is in this world, then God is also being there for us. By receiving the other, we may in some way receive God. Perhaps the strangeness of the other is a paradigm of the strangeness and difference of God from us, a God who in strangeness is present to us.

QUESTIONS

1. What have you experienced in the church that supports racism and that seems to overcome racism?

2. How would you describe your primary world? Your secondary world? From which world(s) do you find yourself exiled?

3. How does your church set boundaries that include or exclude persons?

4. What is your vision for the church of the future and the society of the future? What are some simple and practical steps you or your church might take to move toward that vision?

7 | Ending Racism in Society through the Churches

ALONZO JOHNSON

The other aspect of the issue has to do with the mood, the state of mind out of which discrimination and the response to discrimination come in the first instance. The issue is a moral and spiritual one and falls within the broad and specific scope of morality and religion.[1]

Howard Thurman

HOWARD THURMAN CLAIMS that discriminatory, prejudicial and, by implication, racist attitudes and actions are problems of the spirit—inherently rooted in religion, spirituality, and morality. The seeds of racism, prejudice, and discrimination are first planted and germinate within the human spirit. They represent a diabolical and degenerate violation of the highest ideals and values of the human spirit. To the extent that Thurman is correct—and I believe his insight is utterly true—ending racism in society needs to begin in the churches. To explore this claim, this chapter focuses on three key areas: first, the context of Thurman's vision; second, a definition of the spiritual dimensions of racism; and finally, the institutionalization of Thurman's struggle against racism embodied in the Church for the Fellowship of All Peoples (CFAP) in San Francisco.

THE CONTEXT AND SHAPE OF THURMAN'S VISION

Ideas about God and religious ideals do not emerge from the sky; rather, they are rooted in the personal experiences of individuals and the collective experiences of races and groups of persons. Thurman was a product of the American South. Born in Daytona Beach, Florida, he was nurtured in the South's genteel tradition and victimized by its racism toward and economic exploitation of African Americans. The reality of racism was personal for him as he faced it on a daily basis both in Florida and in Georgia, where he lived during his matriculation at Morehouse College in Atlanta, Georgia.

Saul and Alice Thurman, Howard's parents, were working-class people who gave their children the best they could afford. Saul was a trackman for the Florida East Coast Railroad Company. Alice worked as a domestic for a local white family; the care of her three children—Henrietta, the oldest, Madeline, the youngest, and Howard—was left to her mother, Nancy Ambrose. The family survived through hard work and thrift.

Thurman's theological reflections on segregation and racism did not develop until his final year at Morehouse College. The issue of segregation, especially within religious bodies, was one of the reasons Thurman was hesitant to enter the Christian ministry during his senior year at Morehouse. He was denied entrance to Newton Theological Seminary because of his race. The administration of Newton Seminary, Newton, Massachusetts, advised him that he should instead apply to Virginia Union Seminary, Richmond, Virginia.

He deepened and developed his reflections when he entered Rochester Theological Seminary in 1923, where, for the first time in his life, he was in a "totally white" world.[2] In this context, Thurman began to question his understanding of the teachings of Jesus of Nazareth, especially regarding the racial situation of the times: "How is it possible to believe in the Christian message and not challenge the racial polarization of America? What does my commitment to the gospel suggest about my response to whites? Is a segregated congregation really a church?"[3]

Thurman's response to the problem of racism in religion is provided in his ideas about the life and teachings of Jesus. Thurman posited that churches in the United States had betrayed the religion of Jesus, which, in his opinion, offered an important method for addressing the concerns of persons who must live with oppression.

Racism, discrimination, prejudice, and bigotry are social cancers that eventually destroy every aspect of the social and political fabric of a people. More fundamentally, however, these forces are cancers of the human soul, individually and collectively. They destroy the spirit of a race, a nation, a people, as well as individuals. Thus, segregation is not simply a socioeconomic system; it is "a mood, a state of mind, and its external manifestation *is* external. The root of the evil, and evil it is, is in the human spirit. Laws which make segregation illegal may or may not attack the root of the evil."[4]

As a mood and a state of mind, racism and segregation have their roots deep within the human spirit and psyche. This is not to deny the efficacy of the law in dealing with the social dimensions of racism, prejudice, and segregation, as Thurman went on to note: "Their [law's] great function is to deny the binding character of the external symbol by giving it no legal standing.... The law cannot deal with the human spirit directly. This is not within its universe of discourse."[5]

THE MYTH OF THE GIVEN
AND HUMAN UNITY

Lurking behind Thurman's thoughts on the question of the spirituality of racism and related matters is the strong philosophical notion of the "myth of the given" in human life. The myth of the given is expressed sometimes in philosophical and at other times in theological terms. Simply put, it affirms that there is either a spiritual or an intellectual "core" to human life that is universally present. Thurman affirmed that there is a fundamental common core of human values and components present among all human beings. Moreover, there are core components of the human experience itself, which can again be recognized among all persons.

The most basic component of the structure of human meaning centers on the recognition of the true spiritual kinship between all persons and things in the cosmos. In his 1971 text *The Search for Common Ground,* he spells out the dimensions of this kinship in clear terms. Directly related to this is the human sense of infinite worth of oneself and of all other human beings. When the individual human being is religious, especially a true Christian, she or he is especially called to nurture this insight. The very essence of being human is to "experience" the kinship with other humans.[6]

In *The Search for Common Ground,* Thurman set out to demonstrate that the givens in human life are rooted in the very structure of reality itself. His thesis is that there is a common bond between all persons, living things, and structures in the cosmos. It begins with the fundamental notion of creation itself and extends to the biological, social, and ideological dimensions of the human experience. Likewise, there are common ideals and quests, such as the search for a human utopia, that demonstrate the commonalties between human persons and the nature of their hopes for the future. He saw this, for example, in the myriad creation stories espoused by various peoples.

The key ideas that he drew from the creation myths are their notions of a "creative intent" in the origins of the cosmos, and subsequently in the idea of the unity implicit in this process. If there is indeed a creator, there must be a basic sense of interconnectedness between things in the universe. He went on to suggest that the Creator's intent was that human beings learn to "live in harmony within themselves and with one another and perhaps with all of life."[7] Whether human beings acknowledge this "intent" or the implicit unity in things, the unity is nonetheless present.

The sense of unity in the universe is also manifested in the very concept of life itself. Life is a process, an unending ebb-and-flow movement. It moves from order to chaos, integration to disintegration, harmony to disharmony, but it is nonetheless a rhythmic process. Thurman took this as a literal fact in his understanding of the universe and in his perception of human life. He noted, "Since we are not only living in the universe but the universe is living in us, it follows, then, that man is an organic part of the universe. In his organism he experiences the order and harmony of the universe. In fact, it would not have been possible for him to emerge had certain conditions not been maintained so that life for him and all his multitudinous kinsmen could be sustained."[8]

The implications of these claims, coupled with others that Thurman made in this work, are very clear. Thurman emphatically believed that there is without question a natural kinship between all living things in the cosmos. It is obvious and absolute. Racists, segregationists, and other fascist types are all in denial about this basic truth in the cosmos, but it remains true.

The challenge, then, is to look at specific ways to counter and challenge the deformations of human life, community, and spirit, as are represented in racist and prejudicial actions and activities. In the final section of this chapter, I will examine Thurman's proposal for counteracting the debilitating impact of racism and bigotry by looking specifically at the role played by the Church for the Fellowship of All Peoples in the inception and implementation of his vision of a religiously based program of response to social problems.

THE CHURCH FOR THE FELLOWSHIP
OF ALL PEOPLES

Thurman's nine-year tenure at the Church for the Fellowship of All Peoples began in July 1944. It represents an exact midpoint in his long career in the church and the academy. His career began after his seminary training with brief stints as a pastor in Oberlin, Ohio, and later as a professor and chaplain at Morehouse and Spelman Colleges in Atlanta, Georgia. He spent twelve pivotal years at Howard University in Washington, D.C., where he was dean of the Andrew Rankin Memorial Chapel and a professor in the School of Religion. From Howard, he would go to San Francisco and later end his career at Boston University, where he held several positions on the faculty and administrative staff.

The Howard University/Washington community provided an excellent context within which Thurman could experiment with and test his emerging theological vision. He was always in search of methods and resources for how to address the critical social issues of his generation from a religious perspective. His fundamental conviction was that religion could indeed function as a primary source of power and strength in combating social evil.

In the fall of 1943, A. J. Muste of the Fellowship of Reconciliation informed Thurman of the formation of an interracial, intercultural gathering of believers. The group had come together to break the cycle of institutionally segregated religion in San Francisco. Thurman described his correspondence with Muste as a "fateful" one because it would eventually lead to his departure from Howard University.[9]

Following his conversations with Muste, Thurman began to correspond with Alfred Fisk, a Presbyterian minister and professor of philosophy at San Francisco State College. Fisk had been involved in the formation of a group of religious persons who were interested in beginning an experimental religious community. This community began as a radical idea in that it was to be strongly interracial, intercultural, and interreligious in scope. In his correspondence with Thurman, Fisk broached the idea of Thurman's move to San Francisco to become the copastor of the body that would later become the Church for the Fellowship of All Peoples.

At the very inception of his communications with Thurman, Fisk was clear about the religious and social implications of the organization. He explained to Thurman that the Church for the Fellowship of All Peoples was "the most significant single step that institutional Christianity is taking in the direction of a really new order for America."[10] The significance of the organization centered on its model as an interracial, interreligious, and inclusive community. Fisk, who was well aware of Thurman's international reputation as an innovative religious thinker, used the racial climate in San Francisco in particular and the United States in general as the reference points for discussing the contribution that the Church for the Fellowship of All Peoples could make.

Thurman had gained much acclaim as a conference speaker and religious leader. His 1936 trip to India and meeting with Mahatma Gandhi helped to further his position. He turned the Andrew Rankin Memorial Chapel at Howard University into a virtual spiritual laboratory as he tested his religious vision. He frequently shared his pulpit with both Christian and non-Christian ministers. He was likewise committed to the idea of promoting interracial religious settings where people could realistically discuss social issues. He experimented with such things as liturgical dance and the use of a handbell choir.

Very early in their communication, Thurman caught the spirit of Fisk's hopes and agreed with its implications. He said, "Alfred, we have a profoundly creative, and in some ways revolutionary idea that is fundamental to the genius of Christianity."[11] The specific genius of Christianity was its ability to provide the spiritual and moral resources for struggling against human evil, particularly racism. The basic question for him was determining how religious organizations could contribute to discussions in that area.

Thurman agreed to go to San Francisco in July 1944. He took an unpaid leave from his tenured professorial position at Howard and agreed to become the copastor of the Church for the Fellowship of All Peoples. His salary was a mere two hundred dollars per month, without all of his usual benefits. But he went to San

Francisco because he believed in the principles upon which the organization was founded. His immediate aim was to experiment with the worship and communal settings of the church so as to provide a testing ground for his broader social vision. He said it best: "The Church for the Fellowship of All Peoples was in its essence an attempt to establish empirical validation for what to me is a profound religious and ethical insight concerning the genius of the church as a religious fellowship."[12]

The genius of which he speaks here is rooted in his sense of what is inherent in the religious experience, namely, its healing and unifying powers. He went on to say, "To put it another way, I had to find out myself whether or not it is true that experiences of spiritual unity and fellowship are more compelling than the fears, dogmas and prejudice that separate men."[13]

Thurman's vision was rooted in the idea that an inherent power and resource in the religious experience are universally applicable. He contended that unity and community are fundamental to the human experience and that racism and segregation are counter to the very basic thrust of the religious experience. What he wanted was a demonstration of the fact that religion does indeed foster the creation of community. He assumed that an individual's relationship with other persons is rooted in a more basic and primal relationship with God. In knowing God, one knows the foundations of true community. This is the idea that he wanted to test and put into practice in San Francisco.

The experience of unity, which he believed is the essence of life, is critical to understanding the truth of religion. He described life itself as being based on a "structure of dependability."[14] This structure of dependability has to do with the degree to which all forms of life rely on one another. This is what community is. It is a driving force, a potential. As a potential, community is "on the hunt for that which will nourish it, sustain it and hold it."[15] Community is the actualization of life's inherent potential. Religion helps to affirm and fulfill this potential.

In its theological, liturgical, and organizational structure, the Church for the Fellowship of All Peoples embodied Thurman's vision of an inclusive religious community. It attempted to overcome doctrinal, spiritual, and psychological barriers through the strength of its vision. The early decision to bring Thurman in as the copastor, along with Fisk, his white colleague, was an important symbolic statement about the commitment to racial inclusiveness. Thurman spoke forthrightly about his concerns that the young church should not be divided along racial lines. He noted that they did not want the minority members, blacks in particular, gravitating toward him and the others toward Fisk. His concerns were put to rest; that never happened.

The first governing board of the church, the "Church Board Pro Tem," consisted of five black and five white people. Later the Committee of Nine, consisting of three white, three black, one Chinese, and two Japanese members, was elected and given the task of shaping the goals and directions of the young church.[16]

The membership of the church during Thurman's tenure was likewise inclusive. Of the 350 active members at its peak, 60 percent was of European origin, 35 percent of African origin, and 5 percent of Chinese, Japanese, and Mexican origin. The membership varied along class lines, with most of the members being nonprofessionals.[17] They wanted to test their vision of racial and social inclusiveness in an institutional manner.

Theirs was a quest for a spiritually based, ethically centered religious vision that was broad enough to include all persons. It was by no means a static vision; rather, as Thurman said, it was always testing and being tested. Its testing was the process of seeking to embody a truly inclusive community. There was no push for doctrinal or creedal conformity; the call was for a spiritually based ethical understanding of human community. Because of this basic commitment around which the Church for the Fellowship of All Peoples was organized and continues to function, it could make a significant contribution to U.S. religious history. This commitment also affirms Thurman's place in the discussion of race and religion in the United States.

CONCLUSION

Proper analysis and confrontation are necessary to counteract and eradicate racism, bigotry, ethnocentrism, and oppression. This chapter has presented one specific method of analysis and confrontation. Racism in the United States is more than a social phenomenon; it is rooted in spirituality and religion. It has its own religious meaning, symbolism, and history. The Ku Klux Klan is only one example of the American affirmation of the religion of racism. It is a pernicious, willful evil that seeks to rob human beings of their God-given rights and their privileges as U.S. citizens.

The devastating consequences of racism in the United States are everywhere. We need more than ever to hear Thurman's radical proposal for a spiritually based program of social transformation that is strongly rooted in an experience of true community in accord with the eternal principles of God. Thus, religion and religious experience are the foundations of true community. My hope is that what is said here about Howard Thurman's vision will contribute to the ongoing discussions about race and religion in the United States. I conclude with his words:

> As difficult as it is for experiences of unity to transcend differences of race, it is infinitely more difficult to create experiences of unity that can unite beyond the fundamental creeds that divide. There is an amazing incongruity in the fact that in peripheral matters there is fellowship, there is community, but

in the central act of celebration of the human spirit in the worship of God, the lines are tightly drawn and a man goes before God with those only who believe as he does. The experience that should unite all men as children of one Father becomes the great divider that separates a man from his brothers.[18]

QUESTIONS

1.   Do you agree with Howard Thurman that human beings share a common core of spiritual unity? What are the implications of that belief for the life of your congregation?

2.   How have members of your study group or congregation been affected by their early experiences of racial division or unity? How have those experiences shaped your present convictions and behavior?

3.   If you have ever been a member of an interracial worshiping community, how was that experience similar to or different from that of your current congregation?

4.   What changes might you make in your current situation to move toward the experience of the Church for the Fellowship of All Peoples?

8 | Baptism as Sacrament of Struggle and Rite of Resistance

DEBORAH FLEMISTER MULLEN

As HE TURNED AND SAW THEM following him, Jesus asked, "What do you seek?" (John 1:38 NKJV). They said they were curious about where he was staying. "Come and see," he said (John 1:39 NKJV). In that moment we are able to glimpse the call to discipleship. After some time with Jesus, the two quickly grew to three, then four, and more. "Follow Me," he said (John 1:43 NKJV). And each day another was added. Soon there were too many to count.

The call to discipleship consists of two parts—an invitation and a response. For Christians, it is the most important invitation we will ever receive. Each person must respond for herself or himself in light of the many and different ways this most awesome call comes. Christian tradition considers baptism[1] to be a fundamental response of discipleship, whether administered as an initiation rite to infants and young people or later in life upon the profession of one's more mature faith.[2] In either case, it is rightly understood as an act of the faith community in covenant relationship with God. Therefore, whatever form the baptismal ritual takes, whether administered by sprinkling or immersion, baptism is a sign and universal symbol to the world that the one baptized is on a faith journey rooted in the ministry of reconciliation, death, and resurrection of Jesus of Nazareth.

This chapter is concerned with the question of what it means to follow Jesus and be his disciple today. How do we sort out the meaning of Christian discipleship in an increasingly secularized world, in which the relevance of the church and its ministry is under serious attack, not the least, because of racial divisions among Christians? What role, if any, does or should baptism (as sacrament, ritual practice, or ordinance) play in the lives of those who are seeking the visible unity of the church?[3]

Finally, as disciples of Christ, how do we measure faithfulness to our baptismal vows and renew the commitment to unity as our calling in the midst of a world that has little regard either for what we believe or for the unity we seek? These questions beg our serious attention and thoughtful response if we truly believe that "in sovereign love God created the world good and makes everyone equally in God's image, male and female, of every race and people, to live as one community."[4]

UNITY, FAITHFULNESS, AND RACISM

What does it mean to be the church engaged in the struggle to eradicate racism, a particular form of sinfulness and manifestation of Christian disunity? Given our common understanding as Christians, that in baptism we have received the Holy Spirit as a pledge from God to overcome all that divides us (1 Cor. 12:13), how should we respond to the presence of racism in the churches?

Racism must not be tolerated in the body of Christ because it clearly violates our unity in Christ given to us in baptism. This biblical interpretation of our unity thus forms the basis for the ethical mandate of the churches to eradicate racism. Stated differently, the problem of racism in the church is an issue of Christian "family values." To believe otherwise is to compromise the transformational power of our wider witness to the world as people for whom Holy Scripture speaks an authoritative and unifying word, irrespective of differing traditions or one's particular ideological perspective.[5]

On the one hand, as a social construct, racism is problematic for Christians because it is a perversion of the word of God found both in the Hebrew Scriptures and in the Christian Scriptures (Gen. 1, 2; Gal. 3:27–29). Biblical faith and witness call us to model our common inheritance as "created in God's image" and to affirm that we are joint heirs in Christ's victory over sin in the ongoing struggle against evil in the world (Rom. 6:3–5). On the other hand, racism is problematic for the church as it seeks to represent the visible unity of Christ's body to the world. Instead, our Christian witness remains divided by racism in ways that destroy the world and obstruct the peace and justice for which Christ prayed.

Gayraud Wilmore and other prominent African American theologians have long argued, based on the analysis of Christian history, that "theology has been infected by the ideology of white racism almost from its beginning." This conclusion was included in the first chapter of a document produced by the 1975 World Council of Churches consultation titled "Racism in Theology and Theology Against Racism." Unfortunately, the critical chapter was omitted from the World Council of Churches' official policy statements in 1980, causing Wilmore to wonder (in writing) whether the chapter was eliminated "because it contained one of the most devastating criticisms of Christianity ever issued by an international conference of Christian theologians and social scientists."[6] The fact that the church is divided by racism is by no means news to African American Christians who for centuries have adapted and reinvented a Christianity once distorted by white slave owners and overseers who sought to dominate and oppress them "in the name of Jesus."

Is not baptism compromised, as a sign of visible unity and proclamation of faith, as long as racism is practiced in the church? Put another way, if baptism is the basis of our unity in Jesus Christ, are not racist beliefs and practices among baptized Christians a scandal within the community of believers? Does not the presence of racism in the Christian family pose a stumbling block to those for whom the church's witness is intended to reveal God's unconditional love and justice to all?

BAPTISM AS A SOURCE OF UNITY AND LIBERATION

The struggle to eradicate racism from the church must be rooted in the promises and ethical commitments associated with our baptism, and given fullest expression in our lives through word and deed in ministry and mission. Our profession of faith is radically flawed when we leave unexamined and unaddressed the ways baptism, as seal and sign of the new humanity given by the risen Christ, mandates that we live as though God's saving grace has already been received. Baptism is a source of freedom from all that binds us!

The promises of baptism are good news (Acts 2:38–39; Rom. 6:6–14) and the right teaching by which the whole Christian community may boldly lay claim to Christ's ministry of love, unity, and justice. It stands to reason, therefore, that when practiced in a Christian context, racism is not good news, especially for those who are victimized and oppressed by its false doctrines of racial dominance and white superiority. Racism is sinful false doctrine that must be eradicated from the churches and from the world.

This chapter is an appeal to the churches to examine what baptism "does," to whom and how, and for what purpose(s). It is essentially a critical reflection by "a believer" who trusts the power of the Christian faith tradition to challenge the church to be willing to lose its life to save its soul, and who believes the "church reformed is always reforming."

Whether understood as ordinance, ritual practice, or sacrament, baptism has consequences for the way we live as Christians. Much more can be done within our churches to help members reflect on their baptism as a source of on-going "conversion" to Christ's ministry of liberation and unity and to God's mission to transform the world.

As a woman of color and student of history, I have benefited from biblical, historical, and theological-ethical scholarship distinctly African American and reflective of the black church experience. As a result, it is not possible for me to ignore or minimize the complicity of the churches in allowing the sin and scandal of racism to divide Christ's body. Nor the role that racist biblical interpretation and theology have played in erecting barriers among God's people.

Baptism promises a new relationship between God and the believer (Matt. 28:18–20). Such is the witness found in the Scriptures. This is the gospel truth! It is also the case that the Scriptures have been used to defend the most pernicious and perverse forms of racial hatred, bigotry, and discrimination ever practiced by members of the Christian faith against one another. This sad reality, though discouraging and deplorable, is not the last word, thanks be to God. "For as many of you as were baptized into Christ have put on Christ. There is neither Jew nor Greek, there is neither slave nor free, there is neither male nor female; for you are all one in Christ Jesus" (Gal. 3:27–28 NKJV).

CALL AND DISCIPLESHIP

The ministry of Jesus, whatever else it was, is no less compelling a call to discipleship for today's churches. Jesus moved through life touching persons with dreaded diseases and calling women and men to question the authority of religious and political leaders. He helped sinners seek a deeper, more intimate relationship with God. He showed people by his example how to look within the tradition for truths that would be good news for their lives and disruptive to the status quo of the ancient world around them. Setting forth a radically prophetic vision of a new social order, Jesus turned the tables on the rich and powerful, exposing their sinfulness before God and their contempt for those whom they exploited. Jesus was the incarnation of God's word and passion for justice among people whose religious, social, and economic divisions were a clear and present danger to God's plan.

Jesus came into people's lives giving powerful testimony to God's compassion for the culturally and economically oppressed with whom he shared community in ways that would cost him his life. He invited outcasts to table fellowship, spoke with and accepted the gifts of women, prayed for the healing of Jews and Gentiles alike.

He outraged community leaders again and again as he gave over his life in the service of God's plan to restore wholeness among God's people and harmony among creation. Born Jesus of Nazareth, this human being also bore the divine indwelling presence of God for all time and for every age. His calling and confirmation as God's own Child were truly tested by his trials on earth. His life was ended in death on a cross, but not before his ministry had changed the world!

It is because of who he is and what he did that we are who we are. We are called Christian because of him. Our identity is indelibly tied to the One known to us as Mary's boy and also called Emmanuel (God with us). We call ourselves Christian, thereby making a profession of faith and a promise to accept the terms of our covenant relationship with God in Christ. We promise to live together in unity, observing ways that we believe are consonant with those Jesus Christ modeled in the Christian Scriptures. We call one another Christian as we are welcomed into God's family and give thanks for our new family status given by God as a gift at our baptism. By our baptism we become sisters and brothers, a sign of our already realized unity with one another in Christ under God's plan.

BAPTISM AND MINISTRY

Baptism marks us for a life as disciples of Christ and sets us free to respond to the ministry of "God service,"[7] into which Jesus was initiated at his baptism. Baptism is our initiation into this same ministry and the means by which we take on the full meaning of Jesus' life and death as our calling. Baptism is the way we become heirs with the risen Christ to the ministry of God service and with his risen body, the church, as we strive to reach the goal of visible unity in one faith and common life.

Our identity as Christians was sealed by God in Jesus Christ at his baptism as was the confirmation of ministry as his life work and ours.[8] The Gospels attest to this fact, one of the precious few upon which they agree! In baptism Jesus was "reborn" through water and the Holy Spirit as if to remind all who witnessed of his "mixed" parentage as the firstborn of a woman and of God. Jesus' humanity and his divinity remained commingled throughout his journey from the cradle to the cross. Jesus' sense of himself and his mission rested on his love and fidelity to God, and was bound up with God's urgency to confront the powers and principalities that stood in the way of God's intended dominion of reconciliation and shalom (peace). By our baptism we become participants with Jesus in God's amazing love and radical plan to redeem and transform the earth. By our baptism we take on the burden and the blessing of being the body of Christ in the world.

What, then, does it mean to claim our baptism as a way of truly understanding who we are and what is required of us today? What if being baptized really means we are expected to live together as though the dominion of God has already come? What if baptism really means that our salvation depends upon transcending the divisions among us and our churches? What if we were to decide that we will no longer tolerate our brokenness before our God or allow racial hatred and racism in the churches to deface the image of God in which each of us is created? What if we were to live as though the unity for which Jesus prayed were a reality rather than a goal yet to be realized?

THE MARKS OF CHANGE

Believing that baptism changes the one baptized means also believing that the "condition" of the body of Christ is changed. And while the marks of that change are many, three are critical for any discussion of eradicating racism in the church: confession of sin, conversion of heart, and commitment to new life re-formed by the Spirit.

Confession of Sin (Faithfulness and Struggle)

The "condition" of the body of Christ has long been the subject of critical reflection across lines of theological and sociological discourse within the Christian community. This "body" is in terrible "condition," divided and badly broken by attitudes, beliefs, customs, and practices that separate members from one another. The Christian faith was born of divisions among God's people generations ago, and so it should be no surprise that church-dividing issues, such as racism, have persisted well into the present moment. Historically, racism is both a cause and a result of divisions within the body of Christ. Theologically, it has been a church-dividing and sometimes a church-uniting issue.[9]

There is no room for racism or racial idolatry in the body of Christ! Where racism persists in the churches and is embraced as an expression of faith, Christians must mobilize to restore good faith and order to the whole people of God by publicly confessing racism as sin and renouncing racist beliefs and behavior as evil.

Facing the future means taking on these realities as part of our calling as disciples of Jesus. Racism within the Christian family of faith is incompatible with the gospel of Jesus Christ. The ravages of racism wound deeply and cause permanent disfigurement of the body if left unattended. Baptism is a rite of resistance and sacrament of struggle as we work toward ending racism in the churches.

Conversion of the Heart (Repentance and Resistance)

Racism is a problem of grave consequence for the body of Christ. Whatever its origins and whomever its targets, when racism is ignored, practiced, or tolerated in the church, the faith of the church is attacked and the life of the faithful comes under siege. When racist attitudes and behaviors go unchallenged, are allowed to flourish alongside things held sacred, or become a means by which to express one's relationship with God and Jesus Christ, "Christian racism"[10] is not far behind. Charges of heresy are not too strong a judgment upon such a distorted practice of faith.

We are called to renounce racism if we are truly to be the body of Christ. Our baptism is a sign to the world of our continual need for repentance and reconciliation. The gift of the Holy Spirit at baptism sanctifies us throughout life to receive the unity already given to God's people in Christ. Baptism is a "sacrament of struggle and a rite of resistance" as we work toward ending racism in the churches.

Commitment to New Life (Re-formed by the Spirit)

My main purpose has been to lift up baptism, whether understood as sacrament, ordinance, or rite, as one way to take our common faith seriously and thereby to address the church's unique role in the world vis-à-vis the eradication of racism. Biblically and ethically, our baptism into a common faith and life as Christians offers resources for reimagining the church re-formed by the Spirit to resist racial idolatry and racism. The work of our baptism has been accomplished in Christ! Our calling as disciples commits us to struggle in faith to face those parts of our lives needing to be confessed and transformed so that we might freely receive God's grace and commit to the new life we have already received in baptism.

Baptism calls for repentance from sin and the renunciation of evil beliefs and behaviors associated with racism. Within the household of faith, baptism is the chance to protect children from false teachings of racial idolatry. It is the occasion for children to be publicly claimed by the faith of the church, based on the teachings and example of Jesus Christ, who resisted all that defiled God's love and passion for unity. Baptismal services and rites must become occasions for churches to renounce the evil of racism as sinful and incompatible with Christian calling, faithful discipleship, and ministry in the name of Jesus.

CONCLUSION

Racism is an evil and destructive force everywhere, especially in the life of confessing Christians and the church. Even as it is increasingly clear that the struggle to eradicate racism must play a more central role in the church's quest for visible unity, the churches remain, for the most part, either "white" or "black." It is also true, however, that where baptized Christians and communities have come to confess racism as sin and renounce it as a distortion of the gospel, unity and renewal are being experienced in the body of Christ.

We can and we must begin to live as though our baptism has meaning in our daily lives. We can and we must begin to teach our children by our example to believe the same. If we truly believed that our salvation depended on accepting our common humanity and that in our baptism we accept our differences in Christ, I believe we would sing with the assurance and confidence of saints:

> Join hands, disciples of the faith,
> Whate'er your race may be.
> All children of the living God
> Are surely kin to me.[11]

QUESTIONS

1.   What does the phrase "Christian racism" mean? How is it acted out? Thought about? What makes for these two terms fitting together?

2.   "What if baptism really means that our salvation depends upon transcending the divisions among us and our churches?" says Mullen. How might your church act to transcend the racial, ethnic, class, or language divisions among the churches in your area? Does the local Council of Churches include both mainline and evangelical churches? What steps might be taken to begin conversation across denominational or theological lines?

3.   What choices are involved in being racist as an individual? As an institution? What group within your religious community might appropriately examine your common life to look for racist effects (as opposed to intentions) in your situation?

9 | *The Eucharist and Racism*

TEE GARLINGTON

H OLY COMMUNION, the Lord's Supper, the eucharist—all are synonymous terms that refer to the sacrament in which Christians share in the body and blood of Jesus. The word "eucharist" means literally "thanksgiving" or "to show favor." Although the eucharist was instituted by the Lord himself on the eve of his crucifixion, Holy Communion is also pictured in the Hebrew Scriptures' Passover meal and was foreshadowed in an encounter between the patriarch Abram and the mysterious priest-king Melchizedek.

THE EUCHARIST:HEBREW SCRIPTURES' TYPOLOGY

In Genesis 14, we pick up the story of Abram as he sets out to rescue his nephew Lot who has been taken captive in the ransacking of Sodom and Gomorrah. In Genesis 14:18–24, we witness the Hebrew Scriptures' event that foreshadows the Christian Scriptures' sacrament of the eucharist. Melchizedek, whom scripture identifies as both the king of Salem and the priest of "God Most High," meets Abram upon his triumphant return to Canaan. Melchizedek pronounces a blessing on Abram and serves bread and wine. Abram responds by presenting tithes to Melchizedek.

Many Bible scholars view this encounter as a Hebrew Scriptures' type of Holy Communion. Some scholars consider Melchizedek to be an epiphany, an actual appearance of Jesus Christ in bodily form. Others consider Melchizedek to be a historical figure who foreshadows the combined kingly and priestly ministries that Jesus Christ would embody in the New Covenant.

Immediately following his encounter with Melchizedek, Abram met God again in a most pivotal encounter. At that event, recorded in Genesis 15, Abram's faith was counted by God as righteousness, and God made a covenant with Abram. The sacrifices described in this chapter are all fulfilled under the New Covenant in the Lord's Supper.

Exodus 12 gives us a second Hebrew Scriptures' picture of the eucharist. In our previous example, we left off with the encounter between Abram and Melchizedek. Some five hundred years have elapsed between Genesis 14 and Exodus 12. The descendants of Abram (Abraham) are presently slaves in the land of Egypt. God has sent Moses to deliver the people from their bondage, but Pharaoh has so far refused to release them. Moses calls down nine plagues—God's judgment—upon the Egyptians. Moses issues a final warning: God will visit every Egyptian household, from the greatest to the least, and kill the first-born child. This brings us to our passage in Exodus 12.

God gives Moses specific instructions about what each Israelite family must do to escape the firstborn judgment and have the death angel pass over their house. They should select a spotless lamb, kill it, take its blood and paint it on the sides and top of their doorposts, roast the carcass, and eat all of it. God promises that upon seeing the blood, God will pass over that house and not visit God's judgment there.

Keeping the first Passover was the event that brought the Israelites victory over their Egyptian bondage. It was the event that broke the power of the slave master's whip and caused the children of Israel to walk in God's supernatural provisions. The Passover lamb clearly speaks of Jesus Christ who is declared by John the Baptist to be the Lamb of God who takes away the sin of the world (John 1:29).

The Israelites' exodus from Egypt was also the beginning of racial or national tolerance. The Bible tells us in Exodus 12:38 and in Numbers 11:4 that when the children of Israel departed Egypt, a mixed multitude of non-Hebrews—Egyptians and others—left with them. We can surmise that the Egyptians might also have been welcomed into the homes of the Israelites during the Passover meal and thus came under the same protection.

THE EUCHARIST: CHRISTIAN SCRIPTURES' REALITY

Matthew 26:26–29 is the scriptural account of Jesus' institution of the Lord's Supper. His institution of the eucharist and the sacrifice of himself took place during the Jewish feast of Passover. It is a clear indication that Jesus was indeed the fulfillment of the Hebrew Scriptures' typology—the Passover Lamb, whose blood is the element that causes the judgment of God to pass over the life and eternal destiny of the individual upon whom the blood has been applied. All of the sacrificial laws of the Hebrew Scriptures were fulfilled in the eucharist of the Christian Scriptures.

Matthew 26 records that Jesus has gathered his twelve disciples in an upper room in the house of an unnamed friend who lived in Jerusalem. During the course of the meal Jesus takes some bread, blesses it, breaks it, and passes it to each disciple, saying, "Take and eat; this is my body." He also takes the cup of wine, gives thanks, and passes it to them, saying, "Drink all of it; for this is the blood of the New Testament, which is shed for many for the remission of sins" (KJV).

Although I do not believe that the bread and wine become the physical body and blood of Jesus—the doctrine called transubstantiation—I do believe that a great miracle takes place every time believers partake in faith of the eucharist. There is a great mystery at work here as in all true sacraments given to us by God. Let me elaborate on this as we consider another passage in the Christian Scriptures.

When the apostle Paul wrote his first letter to the Corinthian church, he gave considerable weight to the doctrine of the Lord's Supper. It is clear that it was a sacrament recognized and regularly shared in the first-century church. Acts 2:42 also substantiates this fact by saying that the new Christians in Jerusalem "continued steadfastly in the apostles' doctrine and fellowship, and in breaking of bread, and in prayers" (KJV).

The Christian Scriptures, Eucharist, and Racism

In 1 Corinthians 11:17–34, the apostle Paul gives instructions about the proper attitude and conduct that believers should have in sharing the eucharist. The key verse in this passage is verse 29: "For he that eateth and drinketh unworthily, eateth and drinketh judgment to himself, not discerning the Lord's body" (KJV). This verse is not only the key to understanding the whole passage; it is also the central concept in understanding why racism cannot exist alongside the eucharist. To understand this verse, however, we need to look at several other passages also penned by the apostle Paul.

Consider 1 Corinthians 10:16–17: "The bread which we break, is it not the communion of the body of Christ? For we being many are one bread, and one body: for we are all partakers of that one bread" (KJV).

Hear 1 Corinthians 12:12: "For as the body is one, and hath many members, and all the members of that one body, being many, are one body: so also is Christ" (KJV).

Look at Ephesians 1:22–23: "And hath put all things under his feet, and gave him to be the head over all things to the church, which is his body, the fullness of him that filleth all in all" (KJV).

Consider Colossians 1:18: "He is the head of the body, the church: who is the beginning, the first-born from the dead; that in all things he might have the pre-eminence" (KJV).

And finally, read Romans 12:4–5: "For as we have many members in one body, and all the members have not the same office, so we, being many, are one body in Christ, and every one members one of another" (KJV).

These verses, along with the key verse in the Corinthians passage, are the crux of my argument against racism, which became an issue early on in the first-century church.

Racism is as old as recorded history itself, and it is as current as today's newspaper. In their 1994 book *The Bell Curve,* Charles Murray and Richard Herrnstein present an academic argument on an old theme. Their premise is that certain people are more intelligent or less intelligent than other people based solely on the race to which they have been classified.[1]

Science itself is now questioning the validity of race as a basis of classifying human beings. In a 1989 scientific survey, 70 percent of cultural anthropologists rejected race as a biological category. Currently, scientists are considering the possibility that research involving genes and chromosomes may become a more valid way to classify groups of people.[2]

RACISM IN THE CHRISTIAN SCRIPTURES

Racial or national prejudice on the part of the early church is fairly easy to spot. Consider the passage Acts 6:1–4. Shortly after the inception of the church in Jerusalem, a problem arose: one group of widows was shown preference over another group of widows. The Jews were being preferred above the Greeks. The apostles were quick to deal with the problem. Their solution was to instruct the whole church body to select from among them seven men of excellent character who would make certain that everyone within the large, rapidly growing local church would be treated fairly. That was the birth of the office of the deacon.

Jesus displayed racial or national tolerance in his earthly ministry. Matthew 8:5–13 records the account of a Roman centurion who came to Jesus on behalf of his sick servant. Jesus complimented the centurion for having faith greater than the Israelites had. Jesus encountered a Syrophoenician woman whose daughter was demon-possessed; Jesus rewarded her faith by granting her request (Mark 7: 24–29).

Another passage in Acts gives an even stronger defense against racial prejudice, for it reveals God's viewpoint on the matter. It is clear from Acts 10 that the apostles in the church in Jerusalem were convinced that the gospel message of Jesus' death and resurrection was reserved for Jews only. Jews were to be the only partakers of the New Covenant, and therefore Jews were the only potential church members, they thought. God orchestrated a situation that would begin to change the minds of the apostles. That is what Acts 10 (KJV) is all about.

Cornelius, a Gentile soldier living in Caesarea, received a heavenly vision. In his vision an angel of God told him to send for Simon Peter who was visiting at the house of Simon the tanner in Joppa. Peter, the angel explained, would tell Cornelius what he ought to do. Cornelius immediately instructed two of his servants to go to Peter and ask him to come with them to Caesarea.

Peter, in the meantime, was at his noontime prayer and also saw a vision. At the outset of his vision, the Bible explains, Peter was hungry. The vision, as it happened, had to do with food. Peter saw heaven open and a large cloth descending. Inside the cloth were animals that, according to Jewish regulations, were not to be eaten. A voice spoke, "Rise, Peter; kill, and eat." In his vision Peter responded, "Not so, Lord; for I have never eaten any thing that is common or unclean." The voice answered, "What God hath cleansed, that call not thou common." The same conversation repeated a second and a third time in the vision.

As Peter awakened from his trancelike state and tried to determine what the vision meant, the two servants sent by Cornelius arrived at the house where Peter was praying. The Holy Spirit spoke and told Peter that two men sought him, that they were sent by God and he should go with them.

Peter obeyed, and the next day they arrived at the house of Cornelius, who had gathered his family and friends for Peter's arrival. Peter said to Cornelius, "Ye know that it is an unlawful thing for a man that is a Jew to keep company, or come unto one of another nation; but God hath showed me that I should not call any man common or unclean." When Peter began preaching to the whole group, he further elaborated on his newfound, yet growing, awareness by saying, "Of a truth, I perceive that God is no respecter of persons; but in every nation he that feareth him, and worketh righteousness, is accepted with him."

Later in the book of Acts, Peter referred to these events in chapter 10. The occasion was an apostolic council in Jerusalem. A certain sect within Judaism was still intent upon requiring non-Jewish converts to submit to certain Jewish traditions. The dispute was hot. Peter made an amazing statement: "And God, who knoweth the hearts...put no difference between us and them, purifying their hearts by faith.... But we believe that through the grace of the Lord Jesus Christ we shall be saved, even as they" (Acts 15:8–11 KJV).

This passage shows a remarkable turnaround for the apostle Peter. He had come to the conclusion that there was "no difference" between Jew and Gentile. He had even gone so far as to reverse the order and say, "We believe...we [Jews] shall be saved, even as they [Gentiles]."

WHY RACISM CANNOT EXIST ALONGSIDE THE EUCHARIST

In his high priestly prayer recorded in John 17, Jesus pinpointed the crux of the issue that we are addressing—unity or oneness among believers. Jesus' prayer to God for his disciples—not just the Twelve, but all who would subsequently believe—was "that they all may be one...that the world may believe.... And the glory which thou gavest me I have given them, that they may be one, even as we are one" (vv. 21–22 KJV).

The apostle Paul expressed the same concern for oneness by taking us into the eternal perspective of God. Paul declared in the first chapter of Ephesians that God has intended all along "that in the dispensation of the fullness of times he might gather together in one all things in Christ" (v. 10 KJV).

Do you remember the verses we considered earlier (1 Cor. 11:29; 12:12; Eph.

1:22–23; Col. 1:18; Rom. 12:4–5)? Each of them refers to the body of Christ, which is shown to be the same as the church. Let me repeat: the church that is present on planet Earth, every born-again believer who has been cleansed by the blood of Jesus, comprises the body of Christ. This is not just a literary analogy; this is a spiritual reality.

Therefore, Paul's warning in 1 Corinthians 11:29—"he that eateth and drinketh unworthily, eateth and drinketh judgment to himself, not discerning the Lord's body"—becomes clear. "Discerning the Lord's body" means accepting and receiving all brothers and sisters on an equal basis, not withholding community from some because of racial prejudice. Clearly, the Christian goodwill that we experience in our local church setting will likely be the most personal and intense. But we cannot, we must not, refuse community with any believer on the basis of racial or national origin. To do so would be to violate the warning of "not discerning the Lord's body." Grave consequences—sickness and death—can follow such disobedience.

In the Christian Scriptures, racial disunity was epitomized in the ongoing tension between Jews and Gentiles. Jews were entrenched with the mind-set that they, and they alone, were chosen by God to be the recipients of God's grace. Hear the conclusion of the matter from God's perspective as spelled out in Ephesians 2:

> But now in Christ Jesus ye who were once were far off are made near by the blood of Christ. For he is our peace, who hath made both one, and hath broken down the middle wall of partition between us, having abolished in his flesh the enmity, even the law of commandments contained in ordinances, to make in himself of two one new man, so making peace; and that he might reconcile both unto God in one body by the cross, having slain the enmity thereby, and came and preached peace to you who were afar off, and to them that were near, for through him we both have access by one Spirit unto the Father. (vv. 13–18 KJV)

Herein is the essence of the New Covenant: the Holy Spirit, whose role is to create unity, indwells each and every believer. There can be no discrimination, no prejudice—racial or otherwise—without committing a grievous sin toward the Holy Spirit.

Clearly, God's purpose from eternity past has been to have a people that God has gathered out of "every kindred, and tongue, and people, and nation" (Rev. 5:9 KJV). Once they have been gathered, God surely has intended not that they remain separated by their differences, but that they be united by their oneness in Christ.

In Colossians 1:26–27, the apostle Paul spoke of a mystery that God chose to reveal among the Gentiles. The mystery, Paul said, is "Christ in you, the hope of glory" (KJV). The apostle Peter also received a revelation of the Christ during his walk with Jesus. Peter declared to Jesus by divine revelation, "Thou art the Christ, the Son of the living God" (Matt. 16:16 KJV).

The mystery revealed among the Gentiles is Christ in you. Christ is the head of the church, the Bible declares in Ephesians 1:22 and again in 4:15. It is my contention that individual believers cannot know the fullness of Christ by themselves. It is only together—all believers of all backgrounds—that we come to know and experience the fullness of Christ. If we practice sectarianism or racism in any way, we are limiting our revelation, and we are hurting the whole body of Christ.

Ephesians 4:4–6 declares that "there is one body, and one Spirit . . . one Lord, one faith . . . one God and Father of all" (KJV). Oneness in Christ is a major issue in the mind of God, and it is the basis for believers sharing in the eucharist. Oneness in Christ demands racial unity.

QUESTIONS

1.   Every denomination has a particular understanding of the nature of the eucharist, or Holy Communion. What are the beliefs in your tradition? How are they different or similar to Garlington's tradition?

2.   When you celebrate the eucharist, is yours an open table to which all believers are invited, or are only those who share your particular beliefs included? What are the implications of an open table? Of a table to which those of common belief are invited?

3.   Reread Acts 10 with a group of people in your church. What are the implications of this story from the early church for your situation?

4.   Garlington says that discrimination and prejudice are sins against the Holy Spirit because God's purpose has been to have a people from every kindred and tongue and people and nation. How is your faith community connected with other Christians in your area? In your region? In other parts of the globe? How can you improve those connections?

10 ▊ Violence in the Household
SISTER PAUL TERESA HENNESSEE, S.A.

I BECAME PERSONALLY AFFECTED by and more interested in racism in the 1950s when I was told by an usher in a "white" Catholic church my mother and I were visiting in Washington, D.C., that we would have to sit in the back of the church. I say I was "interested," and of course, I was repelled. That was my first personal experience of racism. The fact that it happened in the church in which I had recently come to full membership left its indelible imprint.

In the intervening years, I went on to become an active advocate in medical and social settings, and I frequently came to assist persons and groups against whom prejudice and racism were the order of the day. Although the work was extremely difficult, there were occasional victories in gaining people's rights and the respect due them as human beings.

When I joined the Faith and Order Unity and Renewal group engaged in the eradication of racism, the old feelings returned, in reverse: I was repelled and not interested in doing any writing on the subject of racism. What good would another book do besides sit on someone's shelf with no effect on anybody? In the meetings, I withheld any offering to write. My concern for people and groups who were the victims of racism was still there. I just was not convinced of the value of writing after having actively advocated for people for so long. Reluctantly, I tried to imagine what I might write about if I wrote anything at all. As I thought more about it, I came to realize that my advocacy could assume a different form. Writing could be advocacy by way of ongoing formation and education.

I am convinced that people can change, can experience metanoia. Christians *can* be different! They do not have to continue being unlike the Christ they profess to follow. Because it is important to have a model by which to understand the dynamics of profound change, I turned to the theory of formative spirituality, which speaks of formation and reformation, and of the participation of human beings as spiritual beings in these ongoing processes.

Racism is a form of violence, a violation deeper than any of the horrors about which we read in our daily news, and these are legion. Racism not only harms a person's physical being; it does violence to the human soul.

PRIMAL ACT OF VIOLENCE

The priest-psychologist Adrian van Kaam has spent fifty years developing formative spirituality. He offers the following description of all violence: "The primal act of violence...is the defensive refusal of the potential fullness of our awareness. It is the denial of the spiritual dimension of our life. All other acts of inner and outer violence against self and others are conditioned by this primal act. This basic violence is the root cause of a blindness that refuses to face the repulsive reality of violent behavior."[1]

This chapter proposes that racism is a most insidious form of violence; that racism is, in the terminology of formative spirituality, a deformative disposition that can and must be reformed. Violence is not an accident. Racism is not an accident. Both are long-standing attitudes, modes of being, at the root of behaviors we have experienced and witnessed far too long. Racism is all the things we have ever known it is. It is alive and well; it is personal and institutional; it is damaging and damning. Above all, racism is a denial of the presence of God, the mystery, within human persons. Racism negates the presence of God in the person treated in this way at the same time it denies the presence of God within the very self of the racist. Racism practiced among Christians, "Christian racism," is surely an oxymoron!

Derrick Bell states that while the challenges to barriers of race are economic and political, they are challenges that "must be resolved initially by the individual." Bell further states, "New and perhaps more effective tactics to combat racism must begin with those who understand that committed struggle, waged with humility and persistence, can bring an inner triumph of the spirit even as, outwardly, one suffers defeat after defeat."[2]

The inner triumph of the spirit requires nothing less than reformation of our inner dispositions. Reforming the violent disposition of racism can and must be resolved initially by individuals. Formative spirituality can point a way for this.

FORMATIVE SPIRITUALITY

Formation theology had its beginnings during World War II in the Netherlands. Adrian van Kaam was a seminarian who, in the last year of the war, found himself and other theology students stranded in the not yet liberated West of Holland. At times he hid from the Nazis in an old farmhouse along with other endangered people from neighboring farms. The young seminarian began to observe how their difficult and painful experiences were affecting the various individuals from different faith and formation traditions. The group included Muslims, Jews, and Christians (both Protestant and Catholic).

The last phase of the German occupation had caused severe losses of families, loved ones, homes, and belongings, along with famine and deportation. The losses caused the group to look for deeper meanings. Van Kaam and the people with him began to discover their own inner resources, their potential for giving meaning to their lives despite the violent circumstances of that hunger-winter. They came to realize that this potency for giving meaning to life, as well as for being influenced by life, was a quality of spirit, of the transcendent dimension of human life.

After the war ended, van Kaam was ordained a priest of the Roman Catholic Church and assigned to the seminary to teach philosophical anthropology, the philosophy of logic and sciences, and a course in the experiential human sciences. He was also invited to teach his formation theology to the working members of the Dutch Life Schools for young adults. During those early years of teaching, he developed his understanding of the human potential for giving meaning to life and world.

Seeing, and Being, in Life and World

Formative spirituality provides a way of seeing self and others, life and world, in the light of who we most deeply are in God. Such a way of seeing spills over into our way of being and becoming and, subsequently, into our way of doing things. Formative spirituality is founded on the insight that what makes us distinctively human is the spiritual dimension. It awakens us to the deepest truths of our human existence and invites us to grow toward spiritual maturity over a lifetime.

We are always in formation. That is, we are being and becoming constantly who we most deeply are in Christ. As we grow toward that spiritual maturity, toward that full stature in Christ of which Saint Paul speaks, we can become more conscious of the truth that we have the potency for forming life and world even as we are formed by them. Opposed to the influences and dispositions that form us into the Christ-form are the influences and dispositions that deform us into the pride-form, of which racism is a very painful example. As Christians, we cannot be idle observers of, or participants in, any type of deforming behavior toward any of our brothers and sisters without endangering our own spiritual formation, our own growth into the One in whom all Christians are becoming who they most deeply are.

Where We Live

Formative spirituality is based on the interformation paradigm, the formation field, that illustrates the interrelatedness of human beings with our Creator, with each other, with the universe, and with life situations. The field of formation has five spheres (see figure 1):

1. Our preformation by the divine mystery is placed at the center of the paradigm.

2. Our inner formation concerns our relationship with God.
3. Our outer formation deals with interrelatedness with other people.
4. The sphere of our daily situation encompasses all its events.
5. The top of the paradigm represents the sphere of our connection with the wider world at large, with the universe.

Our truly human, or spiritual, formation thus takes place within this formation field in interaction with the preforming mystery at the center (for Christians, the trinitarian God), with other people, in and through our daily life situation and events, and in interformation with the wider world.

Van Kaam's paradigm can help us to appreciate our interrelatedness with all of creation and to understand that, as unique and as communal beings, we are engaged in ongoing formation both personally and socially. We are concerned for our private relationship with our God, and we are also in relationship with others and with all of creation.

Formative spirituality can help us to understand that our lives, in order to be in tune with our Creator, must grow in congeniality with ourselves, in compatibility with others, and in compassion for our own and others' human weaknesses. As we mature formatively, our dispositions toward others and the world are also formed consonantly. When we are congenial or are "at home" with ourselves, we desire peace for others and for our world; when we are compatible with others, we want justice for others and for the world; when we are compassionate, we grow in the social or communal disposition of mercy toward others and the world. Again, the unique or personal dispositions to be formed are congeniality, compatibility, and compassion. The corresponding social or communal dispositions are peace, justice, and mercy.[3]

In our formation field, which is indeed the world, the universe, we realize that our relationships are dialogical. We are not isolated individuals. We are indeed formed by the world, by events and other people. God uses human interaction to mediate to us what is God's will for our lives. But we also have the potential to give meaning to our daily life situation and to the world. Each of us can recall persons and events that have influenced us for the good as well as those that have tried to lead us where we should not go. We know that there have been persons in our lives whom we have influenced as well. We are ever reminded that we are not alone in this world and that, as vexing as it may sometimes be, we need one another. Van Kaam's paradigm of the formation field is a reminder of what we profess: that God, the mystery, is at the center of all creation, that we are all made in the image and likeness of God, and that the Spirit of God has been poured into our hearts (Rom. 5:5).

Figure 1. The Human Formation Field

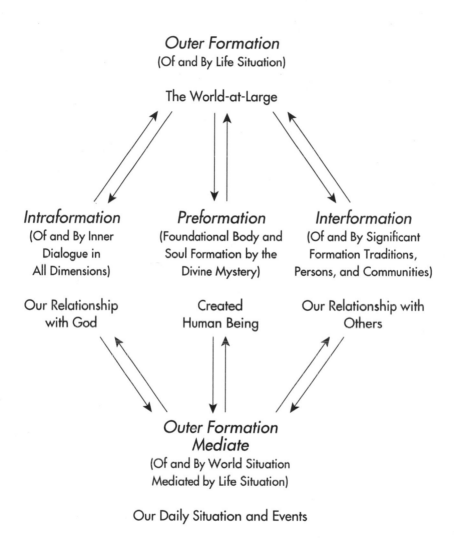

Outer Formation
(Of and By Life Situation)

The World-at-Large

Intraformation
(Of and By Inner
Dialogue in
All Dimensions)

Preformation
(Foundational Body and
Soul Formation by the
Divine Mystery)

Interformation
(Of and By Significant
Formation Traditions,
Persons, and Communities)

Our Relationship
with God

Created
Human Being

Our Relationship with
Others

**Outer Formation
Mediate**
(Of and By World Situation
Mediated by Life Situation)

Our Daily Situation and Events

GOD-NOT-WITH-US

Violence and racism deny the very presence of the Spirit of God within persons on whom we perpetrate these deformative, inhuman acts. Racism and violence demonstrate that the racist, the violator, denies that the Spirit of God is within herself or himself as well. Formative spirituality holds that to be distinctively human is to live in full consciousness of our transcendent dimension, of our souls, our spirits. In and through this dimension we commune with the source, the creative power, the mystery that for Christians is our trinitarian God. In and through this transcendent dimension we are formed in the knowledge of the Spirit of God within us. Van Kaam observes,

> Violence implies a refusal to respect people, nature, and things in their transcendent meaning. It is rooted in a narrowing of our horizon. Instead of walking this earth in wonder, love, and admiration, we begin to live in anxious comparison. We look at others in competitive, envious ways. Such small-mindedness breeds defensiveness, anger, envy, jealousy, and rage. These in turn have to be repressed to make social functioning, or its pretense, bearable.[4]

Van Kaam further states that "repressed violence may turn inward against one's own life or, in veiled ways, against other people."[5] This repressed violence is deformative and therefore is disabling to spiritual, or fully human, formation. Unless the deepest root of such deformation is faced by the person, that is, unless the person comes in touch with the transcendent dimension, the person with repressed violence will continue to live with his or her narrow viewpoint. Violence and racism will continue to be perpetrated on persons who differ in race, color, or nationality.

Being violently disposed toward other persons, becoming racist, does not happen overnight. A disposition toward violence, toward racism, is formed in one's earliest years. A formation tradition in which a child develops deformative feelings of superiority for others because of their race or color is the beginning. As the saying goes, "You have to be carefully taught." A child who is taught to relate to certain other persons from the violent stance of racism and receives no guidance from someone to broaden that narrow horizon of soul will not be open to the transcendent dimension. He or she cannot come to acknowledge the truth that the Spirit of God is present in those persons toward whom he or she is disposed in violence. Neither can such child come to realize that the Spirit of God also dwells within him or her.

TO BE DISPOSED

Experimental psychology uses the word "habit" rather than "disposition." Van Kaam's theory, however, gives preference to the term "form disposition" because it connotes not only the human behavioral aspects but also the ability to learn and live out these aspects. In his thinking, form disposition is a direction or an orientation of character that enables human beings to channel their formative energy into creatively living and growing in life and world. This implies the conscious realization of the transcendent dimension. Form dispositions are considered only relatively lasting because they can change. They can be reformed.

Form dispositions are more than acts. They are the foundation of all our human acts, the direction for human acts. They "dispose us to act coherently and in tune with the direction we have chosen to follow."[6] They are the foundation of our being who we truly are and our becoming who we most deeply are in life and world. According to Van Kaam's personality theory, reiteration (repetition) or formative exercise of dispositions fosters their development.

A deformative disposition is one that moves away from the human transcendent dimension. Distorted perceptions and responses incline us to act in life and world in ways that are dissonant and destructive. Thus, violence is the disposition that spawns acts of racism. The distorted perception that we are superior to certain races or to people of different race or skin color perpetuates the deformative disposition of racism.

"All of us have developed some deformative dispositions. The crucial question is whether we are aware of them and willing to reform them. Otherwise they will keep interfering with the consonant flow of formation."[7] The racist's energies are spent reacting out of deformative dispositions and have nothing to offer to transcendent formation of self or of anyone else.

REFORMING DISPOSITIONS

Deformative dispositions become as much a part of our lives as do formative dispositions, and because of this they have a strong hold over our lives. "It demands more effort to resist or reform them than to learn them. The steady reiteration of the standard sequence inscribes such dispositions more indelibly in our life. The moment we find ourselves in a similar situation, the deformative disposition urges us to repeat the usual sequence."[8]

Because deformative dispositions have often been acquired through relationships with other people, they may be changed more effectively by interaction with others who have the same deformative dispositions. Van Kaam cites movements such as Alcoholics Anonymous in which persons feel supported by others

who are attempting a similar drastic reformation. As in any reformation of deformative dispositions, "the radical disposition of racial discrimination, not simply
its implemental attitudes, must change into racial appreciation if racism is to be
eradicated."[9]

Racial appreciation does not mean being "nicer" to people. Being "nicer" is an
act and does not necessarily mean that a deformed disposition has changed. Reforming the disposition of racism requires a complete turnaround from the deformative disposition of violence that is the foundation for racism.

This reformation means taking a hard look at oneself, at what is blocking the
racist from seeing and from opening himself or herself up to the traditions that
have deformed him or her. It means looking honestly at what in the Christian
faith tradition allowed such deformation to occur. To foster an appreciative disposition means that one sees, believes, and becomes a totally different presence
in one's relationship with God, with other persons and groups of people; a different presence in relationship to the daily events of life and in relationship to the
wider world at large.

The reformation of the deformative disposition of violence, which is the
foundation of racism, requires two human movements. The first is opening to
the transcendent dimension of our lives, and the second is an appraisal of reality
for the truth of who we all are in God. Denying the presence of God's Spirit is
denying the truth we Christians proclaim we live and manifest to the world. "The
respectfulness of the spiritual person is a spring of progress, creativity, and harmony. Violence is a source of evil, ugliness, and regression. Both forces are at
work in us. Violence and respect are contesting forces of formation, constantly
vying for ascendancy in our life. To allow the transcendent dimension of formation to unfold itself means potentially to replace violence by respect."[10] "The
earth is God's and all that is in it, the world, and those who live in it" (Ps. 24:1). It is
not ours to do with God's creation as we will through violent relationships.

As Christians, we are familiar with the reformation of Paul of Tarsus and of
Augustine of Africa. We know of John Newton who, after recognizing his violence and racism, penned in his realized wretchedness the much-loved hymn
"Amazing Grace." Undoubtedly, we can recount more such conversions that followed upon transcendent realization.

But how many more do we need to recall in order to change the picture of violence and racism we know today? What is our Christian response? Or are we
Christians akin to Flannery O'Connor's "Misfit"? Can we not be sure of Christ
and all the meanings of his life for us because we were not "there" with him either? Did not actually see him with our own eyes? Do we Christians truly not recognize Christ, do not see him in others or in ourselves? Is there something in our
dispositions that matches the disposition of the "Misfit"? "Nothing to do but enjoy the few minutes you got left the best way you can—by killing somebody or

burning down his house or doing some other meanness to him. No pleasure but meanness."[11]

The Christian response must be a different one, even while some continue to say we cannot change. Our God and Creator who says, "You have not strengthened the weak or healed the sick or bound up the injured. You have not brought back the strays or searched for the lost. You have ruled them harshly and brutally" (Ezek. 34:4 NIV), is the God and Creator who says, through the same prophet, "A new heart I will give you, and a new spirit I will put within you" (Ezek. 36:26).

QUESTIONS

1.   Can you identify experiences in your daily life that form you toward racial enmity? Toward interracial friendship? How might you change parts of your daily life so that they form you more fully to the new spirit we are offered in Christ?

2.   What elements of your spiritual practice might focus on eliminating the violence of racism? If you do not regularly read materials written by people from another racial or ethnic group, seek some out in your library or a bookstore.

3.   How might your Bible study group develop a study on the deformative effects of racism? Are there study materials in your church library or from your denominational office that have been written by women or men from other cultural contexts? What can you learn from them about your situation and theirs?

4.   What projects or studies might your youth group undertake to examine the effects of racism on their life experience? How are their schools affected by racial division or hatred? What can your church do to address those situations?

PART 3

Anti-Racism Work Across the Churches

11 ■ CASE STUDY:
Struggles in Unity and Renewal Study Group
ANNE P. SCHEIBNER

WITH WHOSE VOICE shall I speak? When I wrote the first draft of this case study about my experience as a member of the Unity and Renewal Study Group, I adopted a consultant voice. Many sentences began with "we" or "the group"; few with "I." Although the group dynamics were clear to me, my role as a white woman was not. I found it difficult to root out my tendency to assume that I could speak for the experience of the group as a whole. Even in the second draft I found it almost impossible to wean myself from speaking from the standpoint of "we" as one of the cochairs.

My automatic tendency to speak for the group now strikes me as being a manifestation of my racism, presenting itself not in the form of an overt statement of my racial superiority but in my assumption of control. Assuming control is something I have been trained to do as a woman of my class and race, and since I always think that I am doing it in the service of the group, I find it socially acceptable.

SCRIPTURAL GROUNDING

Connecting my point of view rooted with my experience of the group did not simplify the question of perspective. Instead, it ended up bringing to the fore the whole question of faith context. I realize now that part of what might have helped me do some real work in Unity and Renewal, rather than participating in trying to make everything nice and everyone comfortable, would have been some serious Bible study.

Bible study was supposed to be part of our spiral of theological reflection and yet for the most part we omitted it. Why? Bible study and explicit reliance on Jesus and the power of the Spirit outside ourselves would have helped me face up to what was happening in the group. Professional competence and personal experience instead were the ground of our work. Prayer and Bible study might have made up for the lack of ongoing skilled outside assistance in helping all of us face our internal dynamics. We might even have been able to name racism in the group not as a matter of shame or blame but as part of the work we had undertaken to do.

Since that time on Unity and Renewal, I have been a member of several parish groups that have used very fruitfully what is known as the African Method of Bible Study. It is a model adapted from the Lumko Missiological Institute of South Africa via South African base communities. It can be used in any situation. First, the passage is read slowly, and a minute of silence follows. Going around the circle, each person identifies what word or phrase jumps out at him or her. Then the passage is read again by a person of different gender. After five minutes of silent reflection, each person tells where this passage is touching his or her life today personally. After a third slow reading followed by another five minutes of silence, each person shares what he or she thinks God is saying to the group based on what that person has heard and shared: How does God invite me/us to change? There is no discussion or dialogue in this process. Each person uses an "I" statement. Finally, each person asks for prayer for himself or herself, another person, or a concern arising from the Bible study. The person on his or her right agrees to pray for that person and concern until the next meeting of the group. When all have spoken, the Prayer of Jesus or some other prayer is said together. This process can take up to an hour and a half, but my experience of it is that the "business" part of the meeting then goes much more expeditiously. As a result one is often finished earlier than would have been the case without the Bible study. The discipline of the method and its requirement of listening carefully, speaking with "I," and praying between meetings I think would have greatly helped our work in Unity and Renewal.

But I now have the ongoing dilemma of how as a white woman to deal more honestly and creatively with racism in the church and in all the groups within which I live and move and have my being. What biblical text would illuminate my present sense of where I stand?

What springs to mind is the story in John 21:1–19 of Peter and several other of Jesus' male disciples in the boat on the Sea of Tiberias. I identify with Peter who, when faced with the question of what to do in the light of the resurrection, decides that it is too hard. He goes back to what is familiar—in his case, fishing; in my case, chairing meetings and writing reports. Needless to say, neither of us caught anything. And now that I can see Jesus on the nonracist shore, I would jump into the water although, like Peter, I would take care to put on clothes because I, too, am afraid to appear naked.

And yet after being fed by the Word, I must answer the same question. "Do you love me?" "Yes, Lord, you know that I love you." And the command is repeated three times so that I may make no mistake: "Feed my sheep." Not with Faith and Order jargon or neat summaries of anti-racist programs. Not any more. "Very truly, I tell you, when you were younger, you used to fasten your own belt and to go wherever you wished. But when you grow old, you will stretch out your hands, and someone else will fasten a belt around you and take you where you do not wish to go." Where was it that I did not want to go during my time on Unity and Renewal, and what was involved in the journey that I did undertake?

Taking My Place in the Boat

When Unity and Renewal decided to focus on race, each member agreed to report on the impact of race on the history and experience of his or her particular denomination. Since many of the white members represented U.S. churches that had divided or, in the case of my church, not divided during the Civil War, this seemed to me to be a fruitful approach. But the final draft of the publication from our previous study on AIDS required more time than expected, so instead of surveying every denomination we began by considering a paper I had written previously on my Episcopal experience.

In that paper I analyzed my experience of race as an issue in the Episcopal women's ordination movement and national church women's organizations. I described my difficulty in identifying myself as a "white woman" and in owning the racial and middle-class biases embedded in my liberal goodwill. Working-class white women and women of color did the child care and housecleaning, which freed me and other middle- and upper-class white women to do church work. In retrospect I could see that the agenda of church "women's" organizations represented primarily the interests of white women.

In the paper I reflected on my experience at a national women's conference at which a panel of black women expressed concerns for a social justice commitment to employment for both men and women and for community safety. Later a panel of white women, which included me, focused on "women claiming their power." The discussion centered on women's inclusion in church governing bodies and clergywomen's deployment. The white women at the conference were upset that the black women could not be supportive of "women's issues."

In the paper I tried to clarify the oppressive racial dynamic that inevitably results from seeing racial justice as a question of "including" one to three people of color on a board or commission made up of twelve to twenty white people. The women's group just mentioned, for example, which had followed precisely that procedure, did not adopt the broader social justice agenda.

One of my assumptions in reworking my paper for Unity and Renewal was that our work would be done from a denominational perspective. In the final portion of my paper, I noted that one person's perspective was clearly not enough. I proposed that Unity and Renewal should ask three to five persons from each denomination to contribute short papers responding to the question, "How has race been a church-dividing or church-uniting issue within your denomination?" My suggestion was not adopted.

Racism Is Alive and Well—Here!

Any effort to deal with issues such as race, and therefore inevitably racism, in a group of colleagues who have various levels of long-standing relationships with one another will be loaded on the side of not rocking the boat. I felt constrained to keep things comfortable for my colleagues as part of my white middle-class woman's concern to "make everything all right" for everyone. I was afraid to point out real differences in how we were dealing with issues of race compared with how we had dealt with sexuality in the AIDS study.

For example, early in our focus on race the group agreed to participate in an anti-racism workshop. During the AIDS study, the group had explicitly rejected the idea of doing a workshop on sexuality. I certainly had no desire to discuss my personal experience of sexuality. But it did strike me as odd that along with the other white people in the group, I claimed to have "no problem" discussing my experience of race and racism.

Following the workshop the study group shifted its focus from race to racism. The group also decided that the experience of the Unity and Renewal group itself in confronting racism would be the basis for our study. At the time the shift from race to racism made sense to me. I do not remember raising the question of whether my proposed focus on race and denominations could or should be pursued. I saw the racism focus as comfortable or at least familiar to the white members of the group, who numbered ten of the twelve most regular members. As a liberal white member of the group, I was loath to protest the naming of racism as our focus, even though I was vaguely uneasy about the shift.

The result of our action was to shift attention to members' individual experience rather than to focus on denominational history and present reality. As one of the three laypersons without academic theological credentials, I assumed that I had gotten the methodology wrong or at least that my proposed denominational focus was not as useful as I had thought it would be. I relied on white feminist theologian Dr. Letty Russell of Yale to be the keeper of the methodological keys and on the black members to be the critical thinkers if such thinking was needed. Instead of challenging the group to think through the implications of the change in agenda, I curled up in my role as cochair and helped facilitate what I took to be the group's new direction.

My memory of the group's reflections on the workshop is that the African American members were much clearer about questioning whether Unity and Renewal should be trusted at all with issues of race and racism. Working on either race or racism as white issues is hard. It was much easier to bury the issues under the cover of the liberal agenda of "addressing issues of race and racism." In other words, I could talk about race and even racism from the viewpoint of being "a person" committed to an "anti-racist" agenda. I cannot recall any of us white members ever identifying how white privilege operated for us in the group. The very fact of thinking of myself as "a person" or "member" and not as "a white person" or "white member" is an example of what I mean. In my case I thought of myself as "co-chair" and not about how my racial identity as a white woman was impacting my perceptions and behavior.

So how was my racial identity as a white woman impacting me? Seven of the twelve regular members of the study group were white women. I was in the majority. But that fact made me feel very uncomfortable about questioning what I took to be our basic assumptions about how to look at the world in general and racism in particular. "Racism, sexism, and classism" has been almost a mantra for my generation of liberal white church women. Very early on, the question of whether we could focus on only one of the "isms" arose. The answer I heard from the white women was no.

For the purposes of the Unity and Renewal study, I was unwilling to say that we should focus on race and not racism. I did not think it was useful to assume that patriarchy was a separate but equal, let alone underlying, analysis. However, I was greatly afraid of being named a gender traitor. Given the composition of the group, I was certain I would lose a battle over basic assumptions before we even began. What I suppressed for two years was that I was interested in the ecclesiological implications of race as a social construction and not in racism as a part of a feminist understanding of patriarchy. When we shifted from race to racism, we stopped identifying ourselves as denominational representatives with responsibilities to our churches and began functioning as "raceless" individuals in a group studying racism.

EXTERNAL AND INTERNAL FOCUS

One way that my racial identity was used in the group was to support the notion that there was no racism in Unity and Renewal itself. Dealing with racism was carefully kept in individual experiences outside the group. Inside the group Dr. Randall Bailey, who is African American and served as cochair, and I were a very visible and glowing demonstration of interracial harmony and cooperation. However, if we had been serious about using the group itself to explore issues of race and racism, we would have had the opportunity to examine whether anyone saw racial overtones in the fact that I listed Dr. Bailey in the lay rather than the ordained column in preparing the final report.

On Not Playing the Denominational Card

Our group homework assignment following the workshop was to engage in "one anti-racist act." I wrote a letter to the newly elected Episcopal bishop of Washington offering to assist him in implementing a pledge he had made to assure that persons of color would be included in the final short list of candidates for rector in all parishes. As a result of the letter, I engaged in a discernment process with a dozen members of the diocese. I was very pleased that my report was later used by the diocesan Racism Commission as part of a study of patterns of parish deployment. However, although I presented the report at a Unity and Renewal meeting, it never felt representative of the work of Unity and Renewal; it felt like my project getting a brief hearing at a Unity and Renewal meeting.

I think my experience with the clergy deployment study is an example of how the idea of using the Unity and Renewal Study Group itself as a case study never gelled. If we had intended to do more than compile a collection of individual experiences, we failed to construct a group vehicle for achieving such a complex goal. I am particularly suspicious of my own plunging into our two years of work so naively.

In addition to having a Master of Business Administration degree, I have training and experience in the study of group dynamics specifically around the impact of race and gender on leadership and authority in organizational settings. Having the training did not make me any less a participant in the covert and overt dynamics of the group. Although I took on a critical and analytical consultant perspective when I drafted the group's final report, I never saw how important was the ongoing lack of reflection on our process. I saw the brief reflection times we had at the end of each meeting as a knee-jerk feminist "we ought to be self-critical" exercise. Certainly if I had thought we were serious about using ourselves as the case study, I would have proposed having written summaries of the learnings and clues from those reflections as the major focus of our meetings and not the individual case studies that in fact occupied the bulk of our time and attention. If I had had to reflect seriously on how I felt the group had used my work in the Diocese of Washington, I think I might have been able to identify how marginalized I felt.

But what other reasons led me to discard the denominational card in which I was clearly very much invested? I was afraid of raising denominational questions that might be perceived as harmful to black church interests. Given my understanding and experience as a white woman of being in an institutional setting controlled by white men, in whose interest was it to overcome racism? Racism had divided mainline white denominations at the time of the Civil War and led to the creation of separate denominational structures for the black Protestant churches. At least those latter structures were not white dominated. Of course, it was the height of intellectual arrogance to think that if Unity and Renewal trumpeted the vision of a nonracial church that the denominational walls would come tumbling down and an undivided church would emerge. Nonetheless, such concerns did give me pause in my urge to press the denominational approach to our study.

I was afraid of stepping on the interests of the members of Faith and Order, including Dr. Bailey who represented a historic black denomination. I spent two years thinking that perhaps there was a good reason why my denominational study proposal should have died. The opportunity represented by the Unity and Renewal Study Group to test whether there could be a nonoppressive vision of a nonracial church was lost. So was the chance to explore whether the historic black denominations now represent an ecclesiastical reality distinct from being simply the effect of racism. But I was afraid of being seen as racist in expressing such questions.

Further Reflections

Several years ago I heard the Honorable Byron Rushing, African American Episcopal state assemblyman from Massachusetts, give an address to the Episcopal Urban Caucus in which he called on white people to give up being white. He also noted that black people should not chuckle too complacently about white people's needing to confront God's demand for justice because the world he was envisioning would require black people to give up being black as well. Any white person who seriously advocates giving up the sorts of privilege—social, economic, and political—that white people have claimed in the "New World" since the fifteenth century may well risk being killed. But giving up being white means at the very least dying to race privilege.

It is helpful to me to see racial identity as something claimed rather than something I am, even though the pitfall is that the privileges are there for me whether I reject them or not. But to think of myself as "being" white is a misnomer and a snare of the devil. My children have helped me realize this truth. Our son Nathaniel at the age of four asked in great perplexity, "How can Mrs. Brown be black?" He also wanted to know what he was, and we decided that "pinkish" was the best description. This conversation should have helped me come to terms sooner with what I thought I meant by "being white." But it has taken longer.

My sense of identity was formed in a society that offered "being white," with all the social, political, and economic privileges that go with it, as the only category for dealing with the physical characteristic of pinkish skin tone. Race has been used not as a descriptive adjective for skin tone, but as a social and political construction to define who is in and who is out of the master and servant classes.

Giving up racial identity in the political, social, and economic sense is not at all the same thing as avoiding it. That passage from John's Gospel ends with Jesus' commanding, "Follow me." White racial identity is certainly a cross to bear. It is not a matter of claiming the German and Dutch ancestries that are part of my heritage. The truth as I have come to know it is that white racial identity cannot be made all right, nor can group distinctions based on race ever be made nice or comfortable. There is one race, and that is the human race. In Christ there is neither black nor white. Can I claim my essential identity as a Christian and let everything else flow from belonging to the dominion of God? Wrestling with the various drafts of this chapter over the last ten months has been a difficult but very useful disciplining process for me. Next time I hope I will have the courage to jump in the water sooner and not worry about rocking the boat.

QUESTIONS

1.   Scheibner stresses the importance of a relationship with Jesus in doing anti-racism work. What spiritual and scriptural resources have you found vital to your work in undoing racism? What steps might you or your congregation take to develop those resources more fully?

2.   The group Scheibner describes worked for two years on questions of race and racism without ever directly addressing their inner group dynamics as they related to race. If your congregation is composed of different racial/ethnic groups, have you ever directly discussed the dynamics of your church as they relate to race? The Guide to Address Racism and Work for Justice found in the appendix is a good resource for such a conversation.

3.   How do you think you would be changed if your church engaged in anti-racism work? What fears do you have about those changes?

12 Conversion, Covenant, Commitment, and Change

RAYMOND BLANKS

TWO HUNDRED YEARS AGO in Pennsylvania, the Christian community in America became a divided household of faith based only on the factor of race. Something strange happened that historic Sunday in 1778 to the small assembly of less than fifty African Americans who were knee bent in prayer at the altar of St. George Methodist Church. Folks formerly bent in roles of subservience suddenly rose erect as they abandoned the white church and separated to journey in an exodus of liberation led by Absalom Jones and Richard Allen.

The Free African Society, the first black religious organization in the nation, involved members who would no longer accept or endure the gross indignities in that Philadelphia house of prayer. In contrast to the white men of the colonial era who had all authority and power in both church and society, this motley fellowship knew deep in their hearts that they were God's children, not God's stepchildren. At the core of their convictions, they affirmed a God who created them in God's image and also endowed them with human dignity and infinite worth as human beings simply because their benevolent Creator was unmistakably present in all of the created order. The separate black church emerged as an alternative to and protest against the racist practices and ecclesiology of the white church. But their equalized experience with God gave them "a special self-identity and self-esteem in stark contrast with the inferior roles imposed on them in American society."[1]

The radical action of Jones, the first black Episcopal priest, and Allen, the founder and first bishop of the African Methodist Episcopal Church, is now a matter of history largely ignored by church historians. Yet two centuries later, the church must still struggle because it has not reduced significantly the repugnant residue of racism. The resurgence of racism requires people of faith to continue the exploration and examination of the persistence of racism, which remains deeply embedded within our ranks and in the wider society and, more important, denies God's plan for creation. Racism, as a dimension of moral decay in our society, significantly limits, distorts, and retards the mission of the church.

RACIAL DIVISIONS IN THE CHURCH

The article "Mainlines and Minorities" in the *Christian Century* reported that efforts by mainline churches to reach out to people of color sometimes produce as much ill will as understanding. The article further indicated that evangelistic efforts to attract minority members can backfire and cause new tensions rather than allay old ones. This brief report captured well the current conflict centered on color, culture, and Christ facing our churches and the nation. The article noted that "the racism at the heart of separate churches is so entrenched that any meaningful multiculturalism is many years off";[2] it remains only a dream, a future hope. Equally disturbing were the reported attitudes of blacks and whites regarding the development of a multicultural body of Christ. Black Christians view the multicultural effort by mainlines as another effort of domination by whites in an era of declining membership. White leaders maintain they will continue to encourage churches to strengthen their ministries and memberships by becoming multicultural.

The article further noted that the paucity of participation of blacks, for example, in several mainline churches indicates dismal results. Blacks are 5 percent of Episcopalians, 4 percent of Lutherans and Southern Baptists, and 3 percent of Roman Catholics. The number of blacks as ministers in those mainline denominations is equally scant. People of color in seminaries remain less than 5 percent of total enrollments while our nation's president has more high-ranking black administrators than all of our mainline denominations. Such disturbing data and descriptions regarding demographics of people of color suggest cogently that the church must become more deeply committed and engaged in acts of internal healing before it can, with integrity and influence, impact the secular society regarding the persistence of racism.

The Christian community urgently needs to halt the hypocrisy and hot air in its discussions about race and religion if the church is to claim the truth and be society's thermostat rather than merely its thermometer. The universal church of Jesus Christ must, of course, strive to be multicultural. Theologian Larry Rasmussen admonishes Christians regarding the reality of racism in saying that "people who are supposed to know something about sin . . . had best recognize how subtle and deep this human demon is, this demonic tendency to think ill of those we disadvantage and oppress because it helps keep us from the stark truth of our ways and the stark truth about the edifices that support those ways."[3]

In tens of thousands of our churches across the nation, regardless of denomination, only a few dozen people of color serve as pastors beyond inner-city churches, are deans of our seminaries, or hold executive positions in our denominations. In an era when minorities are nearly one-third of the college cohort, most religiously related colleges and universities have minority enrollments of less than 10 percent. Racism in religion is even more apparent when we consider those of our ranks, like judges in our courts, who ignore the requirements of justice, doctors who refuse to treat publicly assisted patients, bankers who are firmly committed to loan policies of redlining, or police officers who brutalize only those targeted for selective persecution.

THE NEED FOR CONVERSION FROM THE SIN OF RACISM

I have made reference to the *Christian Century* article and offered evidences of racism's vitality among Christians not to depress or to cause guilt. It is, rather, more helpful if we see the practice of racism as a need for our continuous conversion as Christians so that we might all become more fully human and more fully Christlike. The church needs to be healed of this poison of racism if it is to be a source of healing for our society. We must acknowledge that if Christians in the United States, and only Christians, ceased participating in racism, this problem would be radically diminished in our churches, homes, and society.

Racism as used within the context of this reflection is a form of idolatrous faith that the dominant group uses to assert superiority in order to subordinate another racial group. It is a system of meaning and values that alienates the human family. The racist mythologies, or lies of the majority, assume and assure that people of color are deficient or defective and dangerous, and therefore should be dominated and made dependent.

Racism is a sin because it divides humanity, denies the dignity of all persons, and distorts the human worth of all of divine creation. Racism reflects the fact that some people overestimate their worth, achievements, and abilities with astounding arrogance. In effect, racists prefer to be slaves to their ideology of superiority rather than exist as God created humanity, for community. Racism, as sin, makes apparent our need to repent in order to be freed from ourselves, to turn our lives over to the Divine Redeemer who alone can save us and transform us. In effect, a sin such as racism hinders all people from becoming what God created all humanity to be.

The gospel makes cogently clear that God's Spirit changes individuals, and that social change is also ultimately realized through individuals as God's witnesses in the world. This dynamic is commonly referred to as conversion. Both the Hebrew Scriptures and the Christian Scriptures declare that there is no gap between turning to God and our service in transforming the social order, between our personal struggles for salvation and our work within the world. Our personal relationship with God is made real in our service to our neighbors. We should not discount the fact that Jesus' call to repentance is immediately followed by his invitation to discipleship.

Biblical language regarding conversion always speaks of a turning from and a turning to, a metanoia, of losing oneself and only finding one's true self in surrender to God's will through works of witness. The final goal of conversion is the restoration of the dominion of God in the whole creation. Conversion is our human response to God's call to participate in God's mission in the world. This discussion focuses first on personal spirituality because we must understand the necessity of continual conversion before we can contemplate or create a community without racism. We desperately need to live with an echo of Peter's word regarding conversion: "Repent therefore, and turn to God so that your sins may be wiped out, so that times of refreshing may come from the presence of God" (Acts 3:19–20).

Mary

The vertical and horizontal dimensions of a profound spiritual conversion are captured powerfully in the witness of Mary. Once she was overshadowed by the Holy Spirit, she consented to cooperate fully in the work that God required of her. Thus she exclaimed, "Let it be done unto me." She did not consider whether what God required of her was popular, whether it would financially enrich her, or whether it would increase her social status or political influence. She turned toward God in order to strive faithfully to be obedient to God's will, and she realized the blessing of being God's and therefore proclaimed, "I am the handmaid of the Lord." Through her conversion she could claim her connectedness not only to God but also to her neighbors. Her conversion was the source of her identity and determined her life's direction. Mary knew that the serious servant must testify by both life and works. She was committed to God's message and mission, yet she was fully focused in her faithfulness to God's afflicted people. Her soul magnified the Lord, but she also knew that her conversion enabled her to serve God through others according to the promises of the covenant.

Conversion Is Personal and Social

Christian conversion never involves a division between personal spiritual illumination and a commitment to building a more just society. No conflict exists between prayer and action. A clean heart and a right spirit empower us to stand against the principalities and powers to proclaim Christ. Conversion can be ultimately recognized by the fruits of our labors. Conversion is linked with entry into the church and also enables the faithful to serve Jesus' cause in the whole creation, including those among us of low degree, "the least of these," with hair like sheep and hues like the earth.

In the Nairobi Assembly of the World Council of Churches, the final document on conversion, "Confessing Christ Today," stated:

> We deplore cheap conversion without consequences. We deplore a superficial gospel preaching an empty gospel without a call into personal and communal discipleship. We confess our own fear of suffering with Jesus. We are afraid of persecution, fear, and death. . . . We deplore conversion without witness to Christ. There are millions who have never heard the good news. . . . We find it more comfortable to remain in our Christian circles than to witness in the world. . . . We regret all divisions in thinking and practice between the personal and corporate dimension. "The whole gospel for the whole person and the whole world" means that we cannot leave any area of human life and suffering without the witness of hope. . . . We regret that some reduce liberation from sin and evil to social and political dimensions, just as we regret that others limit liberation to private and eternal dimensions.[4]

Conversion, this ecumenical group advised, is the power of God to change lives and to make all things new. The urgent demands of the dominion preached by Jesus and exhibited in his personal example indicate that personal conversion must also be associated with social praxis. The just are those who do works of justice. Personal justification is inseparably linked with works for social justice. The conversion required of Christians calls for us to realize a re-creative justice that restores the broken community. We are to become just as individuals and to do works of justice in spheres beyond the sacred. Through our conversion, we discover that believing in God is not only loving life but also working as God's servants so that life will be abundant for all.

The two aspects of conversion merge as we become engaged in a fundamental change in our interests and moral values and put ourselves in service to God's dominion. As we give up our ideas, our idolatries, and even our very lives, love emerges as our highest value in life. Once we are drawn into the orbit of Jesus' love, we are able to witness to the love that saves both sinners and unjust systems. Only the power of Jesus' love can touch us beneath our racism and alter our illusions of pride, making us strangers to the persistent sin of racism.

COVENANT

The biblical concept of covenant further encourages us to act in ways consistent with God's plan. The covenant expresses a profound union, a partnership and relationship between God and all humanity. Ain't it good news that we don't have to fight the powers alone—the forces of racism—but that God is still with us? Through the sacrifice of Jesus on the cross, the New Covenant enables us to share in God's sphere of life. We should never forget that we are the heirs of the One who promised as our Good Shepherd to restore us and to turn us from our evil ways and redeem the times. God announced from Genesis to Revelation the divine covenantal steadfast love: "You shall be my people and I will be your God."

Through the covenant, we are reminded of our lives in the grace of Jesus who separates us from ourselves and the world, and yet compels us to assume our responsibility to and for the world. The Christian life is, as Saint Augustine suggested, a "covenant of grace." The covenant is a sign that God condescended to come among us so that we might discover the fullness of our humanity and enjoy the benefits of community. God remains in the midst of us and our struggles for justice, mercy, and righteousness because God remains fully committed to the divine-human covenant. By word and deed, through God's declarations and actions, we have been chosen and graced for a permanent relationship based on the faithfulness of God's promise.

Because of the covenant, God keeps calling us and drawing us to the divine purpose for the whole creation. It is only a matter of time before we shall celebrate God's victory over the forces of sin and evil, including the persistence of racism. Slaves used to sing, "I'm so glad troubles don't last always," because they knew who held tomorrow. The ultimate power of love expressed in the covenant is the same power that will yield an ultimate victory in the triumph of reconciliation over our separation caused by sin. Anchored in God's will, we may yet be able to move beyond conversion to covenant commitment, and thereafter to realize justice, to foster reconciliation, and perhaps to even experience more deeply love for God and our neighbor.

This same covenant influence will also enable us to see the necessity of working ecumenically as a coalition of conscience in combating racism. If we are to reverse current trends of rising racism, then we must join forces. Blacks and whites, younger and older, Protestants and Catholics, and people of other faiths should cooperate in order to realize systemic changes and the benefits of justice for all. Such unity among us with focused leadership can contribute to and sustain our battles against racism. We can become so much more wonderful as servants seeking justice than we ever imagined. This unity of the faithful was briefly displayed by the church in the struggle for civil rights thirty years ago, and it created profound systemic changes.

COMMITMENT AND CHANGE

It is critical to understand that the new racism today is both structural and attitudinal. The systems that control the lives of many have been organized by the few to keep people of color in their place, at the bottom of the social heap, outside the main arena of action. Negative projections, caricatures, and myths about the depravity and degradation of people of color persist at a time when we are increasingly diverse demographically and the nation's economic strength is also increasingly dependent on the gifts and contributions of all citizens. Faced with a huge deficit, high unemployment (the national rate is 4.3 percent, yet the rate for blacks is 8.9 percent), decreased federal spending in the social sphere, increasing levels of homelessness, the demise of the family, diminished urban centers, and the failure of our schools, we must acknowledge that racism, although more subtle, is today not a merely political issue but has particular impact on the economic sphere.

We may certainly crush the mythology that supports the assumptions of those who value themselves as superior. We cannot ignore, however, that economics have always reflected our divisions, with whites employed in lucrative professional positions and people of color employed in the service sector. Gross economic inequality is further reflected in the income gap between whites and people of color, which remains 60 percent that of whites.

Commitment

Dismantling racism, therefore, requires more than debunking white lies. Christian principles of economic justice must continue to be focused especially on poor people and persons previously excluded from the economic mainstream. It must also include a willingness to sacrifice so that many may have enough to live in dignity. Racism's demise will be more apparent when we see increased levels of economic equality and opportunity and smaller income gaps between the haves and have-nots in our society.

In this era when many Christians are confused about their vocation and many people are threatened by economic stagnation, sound communities are facing moral decay, the anarchy of the underclass, the terror of violence, the fear of crime, and the practice of public deceits. In such paradoxical times, we must still inquire about how we are to respond as witnesses of faith in a fear-filled and self-centered world.

A distinctive strength of Christianity, maintains the philosopher Cornel West, is "its promotion of an unstoppable predilection for alternatives grounded in the present." He further emphasizes that

> the Christian tradition, despite its vast complicities with dogmatisms, cynicisms, and status quos of old, contains the resources which enable us to build upon and go beyond the present. To put it crudely, these resources are: the indispensable yet never adequate capacities of human beings to solve problems...; the good news of Jesus Christ which empowers and links human capacities to the coming of the kingdom—hence the warding off of disabling despair, dread and cynicism and death itself; and last, the moral claim to view all human beings as having equal status, as warranting the same dignity, re-

spect and love, especially those who are denied such dignity, respect and love by individuals, families, groups, social structures, economic systems or political regimes—hence the Christian identification and solidarity with the downtrodden and disinherited, with the exploited and oppressed.[5]

Our hope and strength in the struggle against racism and injustice are still to deny ourselves, discard our attachments to idols, and plead the cause of Jesus Christ through our constant service to humanity. Christian faith affirms consistently the primacy of community and the sacredness of life in its fullest dimensions. When we seek Jesus, the vision of our hope will be made plain. We will see not only with our eyes, but also with the advantage of faith that enables us to depend solely on the Sovereign who is the source of our power that sustains us in our commitment to implementing world-changing plans. We are called not to achieve results but to be faithful to the service demands of the covenant.

Change

Our goal in dismantling racism is to set free the victims of racism and to free the oppressor. We seek not only our own reconciliation to God but also the reconciliation of the world. We must discard our attachment to idolatry and break the power of the idolatries binding us. Ultimately, our purpose in this struggle is to set free all people from sin, including racism, and to live recognizing God in all people. This is our task because the elect acknowledge that humanity was created for freedom. Jesus came into the world to set at liberty people oppressed in personal sin and by sinful structures and systems. Michael Kinnamon reminds us regarding this fellowship of faith set free by the covenant and the cross that

> in a world that is so desperately enslaved, so firmly enslaved that it doesn't even know it, the church is a freedom movement. To those whose lives are distorted by greed and pride, the church is a freedom movement. To those whose lives are diminished by the greed and pride of others, the church is a freedom movement. To those whose lives are stunted by fear and mistrust and envy, the church is a freedom movement. . . . To those who divide the world into us and them, the church is a freedom movement.[6]

There are people who now act free because they realize that all people have been set free by Christ's cross. The dominion of God began anew on the third day, and it continues to reveal itself in the midst of suffering and sorrows. God's gracious and glorious power has already been manifested. The benefits of Christ's sacrifice remain powerful and are further revealed by victims of racism who affirm their own dignity without denying the humanity of oppressors. The continued struggle for justice is evidence that God's purpose will win against all odds or any opposition. Resistance to racism by Christians remains a sign of hope. The powerless and excluded already realize that they are somebodies in God's sight because they have discovered within themselves the resources graciously gifted to all in creation.

CONCLUSION

The battle continues, but the victory has already been won. One day the faithful shall rejoice with the saints and exclaim not merely "we shall overcome" or we are "free at last" but "the kingdom of the world has become the kingdom of God and of God's Messiah, and he will reign forever and ever" (Rev. 11:15). The faithful shall rejoice because the One who had all power in the beginning still rules as God who makes us all a new creation and transforms the world into the New Jerusalem. Christians need not get weary because we strive to serve the God of life. We need not be discouraged because the forces against us are strong and have shaped the social system to their benefit. We need not surrender to the ways of this world or become beguiled by the deceits of the dominating powers. We should instead look up and see our Redeemer drawing near. "Do not weep. See, the Lion of the tribe of Judah, the Root of David, has conquered" (Rev. 5:5). We can continue our battle of combating racism with a confident hope, being faithful to our call, conversion, and covenant commitment. The world shall know that these radical alterations, including our personal salvation and the world's social transformation, have been won by God's hand.

QUESTIONS

1. Blanks insists that conversion must be both inward and outward, that prayer must be accompanied by works. When have you experienced a fundamental internal change around any issue that resulted in altered behavior? What might help you be converted around the issue of racism?

2. Many churches have covenants for their members that include statements of belief and action. If your congregation has a covenant, read it again in light of Blanks's comments on the divine purpose for the whole creation.

3. Blanks reminds us that Christians have an alternative perspective, a countercultural vision of wholeness, dignity, respect, and love, that gives us God's strength in the midst of our weakness. How have you, or your congregation, experienced this strength from God when you have identified with downtrodden and disinherited persons?

4. Has the gospel given you freedom? If so, how has that freedom been evidenced in your life?

13 | A Call to Move Beyond the Heritage of Christian Racism

RENA KAREFA-SMART WITH GORDON E. TRUITT

IN THE LATE TWENTIETH CENTURY, Christian churches are on the verge of a new era of visible unity in which the basis for association is justification by faith, and life in the "new creation" is renewed in eucharistic sharing. Affirming that the community of God's people in the churches for the world is the community of all those by whom Christ's redemption is freely accepted, Christians everywhere find that the challenges of seeking to live as such a koinonia community are broad and deep.

Koinonia calls the churches to refuse to live any longer as racially defined and divided communities in a racially defined and divided world. Further, koinonia calls the churches to eradicate this "sin," "heresy," "evil," "menace" of racism-caused suffering. In the following pages I will examine the development of Christian racism, outline an approach by the World Council of Churches to the issue of racism, and offer a model of Christian social ethics through which churches can be transformed by Christ the Reconciler into eucharistic communities whose identity is that of brothers and sisters in Christ.

DISCOVERING ROOTS

The concept of "race" has undergirded a belief system that has made it impossible for churches to move into koinonia communion. In the twentieth century, the churches have become increasingly aware that Christian racism, the particular burden of churches in northern developed countries, is alien to the gospel. The ways in which churches have responded to racism in society within and beyond the church have made us even more conscious of the ways in which our history has supported and promoted racism. In this century the churches have taken three approaches to racism: a time of "resolutionary race relations" (from the 1920s through the mid-1960s); the "struggle for racial justice" and the Programme to Combat Racism (1960s through the 1980s); and the current era of the "eradication of racism" and the movement beyond Christian racism to envision and create a nonracial church and world. Each of these approaches has led us into a deeper examination of our own history and the role that racism has played in forming the churches, leading to the inevitable conclusion that, for the life of the world and the churches, Christian racism must die.

In the first half of this century, ecumenical meetings provided a forum in which church leaders explored the "problem of race relations." Drawing on a long history of Christian reflection on the reason for various "races" and languages, these leaders placed a positive interpretation on the phenomenon of race, viewing the diversity of peoples as a gift from God intended to enrich all of humankind. Such diversity naturally caused tensions when various "races" shared the same city or nation. So churches focused on the tensions that signaled the need for amelioration of discriminatory practices by white people against people of color. National bodies and the World Council of Churches took strong positions on racial equality, infringements against racial justice, and such "critical issues" as the German National Socialist Party's doctrine of Aryan racial superiority.[1]

The end of European colonialism after World War II gave rise to anti-Western sentiments among African and Asian peoples as well as to strong new nationalist movements to preserve European dominance in places such as the countries of southern Africa. Militant African American movements challenged the relatively complacent attitude of U.S. churches. These growing confrontations forced the churches in the United States and in other countries to see race not only as a gift of diversity but also as a politically charged issue. Discussions about the use of violence and nonviolence appeared on the agenda of church meetings. Increasingly, too, the churches began to examine their own histories and the ways in which theories about the dominance of European civilization had been incorporated into their missionary agendas.

In 1969, the first General Secretary of the World Council of Churches, Dr. W. A. Visser t'Hooft, noted the churches' overreliance on "persuasion," their failure to see the primary importance of economic factors, and the costly nature of the sacrifices required for advance. He also saw that the failure to agree on methods of change (violence/nonviolence) was a deterrent to effective action by the churches. To move them toward a more focused approach, he called attention to the Reformation position affirming the right of resistance against tyranny.[2]

Dr. Visser t'Hooft's challenge was a factor in the shift to the second phase of opposition to racism: the struggle for racial justice and the World Council's Programme to Combat Racism (PCR).[3] Given the location of the churches that participated in the program's development and the realities of colonial imperialist history, the struggle was described as opposition to "white domination" or "white racism," and the challenge was to achieve social justice between the "races."[4] Issues of power—its definition, transfer, and defining role in the system of white racism—were central to the typological analysis of all forms of racist oppression. Increasingly throughout the 1970s and 1980s, the liberationist theological method of action/reflection came to shape the approach to the issue. The churches sought to create new models of solidarity and witness that would place them at the center of societies in which racism was a destructive but enduring evil.[5]

This struggle led the churches to a discovery of just how deeply embedded racism was, particularly from the perspective of Western Christianity, in the sources of European Christianity. We came to find woven into our very language of prayer attitudes of racist superiority. We found it hard to pray with the psalmist, for instance, that God would wash away our sins and make us "whiter than snow" (Ps. 51:7) because we heard that phrase as a challenge to our awareness of the colors of the people around us. (In fact, for just such reasons, the Episcopal Church changed the translation of that psalm in the 1979 Book of Common Prayer so that it prayed that God's grace would cleanse the psalmist, and "I shall be clean indeed.")

We also came to recognize that even our titles for non-European and non-Christian peoples were rooted in racist attitudes as deep as the alleged superiority of ancient city dwellers over their country cousins (pagans), the Roman Empire's view of conquered nations in which the inhabitants spoke a strange-sounding language (barbarians), and ancient hatreds between the Anglo-Saxons (heathens) and the conquering Normans.

Such a growing awareness of the deep roots of systemic racism shook church leaders and led them to see a demonic force at work in racism, as in this statement by the Central Committee of the World Council of Churches during a meeting in Canterbury:

> Our struggle is not against flesh and blood. It is against the principalities, against the powers of evil, against the deeply entrenched demonic forces of racial prejudice and hatred that we must battle. Ours is a task of exorcism. The demons operate through our social, economic and political structures. But the root of the problem is as deep as human sin, and only God's love and man's dedicated response can eradicate it. The World Council's programme is but part of that response. It is God's love and not the hatred of man that must ultimately triumph. By God's love, by the power of His Spirit, some day, soon, we shall overcome.[6]

In a later statement, the council made the point that "what is at stake is not just the future of a programme, but the integrity of the Church's life and the credibility of our witness to Christ as Lord of all."[7]

The issue was shifting from a critique of society beyond the churches to a recognition of how deeply the churches needed to repent of their racist past and present. If they were to be credible witnesses to the gospel, the churches were coming to realize, they must combat a racism that was woven into the language and attitudes of Western Christianity. The authorization by the World Council of the Programme to Combat Racism represented the churches' intention to become a credible, ecumenical witness in the struggle against racism.

> The five-year program included a Special Fund to assist groups of the "racially oppressed" in their struggles for liberation. The regular funding for the program was provided by the churches from the operating budget of the World Council. It was agreed that as PCR was a sacrificial effort, the churches were to be directly responsible for its funding. The 1969 adoption of the program was renewed in 1974. It has continued as one of the most effective of all the ecumenical initiatives. However, it is still a very controversial undertaking.[8]

The struggles about the Programme to Combat Racism led finally to a perspective that is directing the current witness of the churches against the racism that has been communicated as part of the Christian message. An analysis made in the years before the Programme to Combat Racism offered theological clarity to the churches' mission "to combat racism." George Kelsey's seminal work *Racism and the Christian Understanding of Man* related historical and ethical themes in a new framework for the current direction of the ecumenical churches' witness against what may be called "Christian racism."[9]

At the end of the twentieth century, we have come to recognize that racism in the West is rooted in religious intolerance that goes back at least as far as the Middle Ages and perhaps even to the expulsion of Christians from the synagogues in the first century C.E. Religious rivalries among Christians, Jews, and Muslims resulted in group alienations that were structured by slavery, persecutions, and war. Believers and unbelievers were in constant conflict. As George Kelsey summarizes the period, "Christians enslaved Moslems, and Moslems enslaved Christians. Both groups enslaved pagans, heretics, and Jews."[10]

In tracing the development of Christian European racism alongside European colonial expansion, Kelsey notes that the first European colonizers did not consider Africans to be less than human because of their physical features, but because they were "infidels...outside the pale of both spiritual and civil rights."[11] Church officials tried to ameliorate such attitudes by demanding that, along with the right to conquer and enslave "infidel" nations, the European armies would have the duty to convert their captives to Christianity and then manumit those who accepted conversion. Not surprisingly, conquering nations made little effort to support or encourage the equality that theoretically followed on conversion of subject peoples.

Gradually, for economic gain, both the church and the nations shifted the grounds of European superiority from religious to racial grounds. The need for an inexhaustible supply of cheap labor was met by the "formulation of an ideological justification for political and economic interests."[12] In time the system became one that resulted in "estrangement in the order of human beings as such. . . . It [divided] human beings . . . along a line which is not primarily a cultural, political, or economic boundary." This system came to issue "declarations of faith . . . not assertions of facts or empirical generalizations . . . that the in-race is glorious and pure as to its being, and out-races are defective and depraved as to their being."[13]

This approach, once in place, sought for and found justification in a racist reading of Scripture ("You are a chosen race . . ."), in the ethnocentric attitudes of Greek and Roman antiquity, and in the "logic" of a Eurocentric anthropology developed when colonialism was at its height in the Age of Enlightenment.[14] Finally, the power of this racism led to a judgment among European Christians that "God has made a creative error in bringing out-races into being, as they are defective in essential being, the victims of a double fall." Kelsey continues,

It is an anomaly that morally concerned Christian leaders rarely understood racism for what it really is . . . racist ideas and practices were viewed by morally sensitive Christians as nothing more than expressions of cultural lag and as products of ignorance. Since racial hostility is one of the forms of human conflict, many Christians have sought to understand racism wholly in terms of political, economic, and cultural factors. They have not seen the faith character of racist devotion and commitment, nor that racial antipathy is conflict in the order of humanity. A probable explanation of this peculiar state of affairs is that modern Christianity and Christian civilization have domesticated racism so thoroughly that most Christians stand too close to assess it properly.[15]

Professor Kelsey's analysis illuminates key aspects of Christian racism. His thought also prompts churches to be proactive in a world that still suffers from "racial" division. The search informed by this perspective continues for an approach that will finally eliminate Christian racism from church and world.

BEYOND OUR ROOTS: FOUNDATIONS FOR A NEW VISION

Christian racism has prevailed as an organizing principle of church life for another reason: a faulty ethical method. The use of the unscientific notion of race has resulted in an ethical method that has failed to identify the fatal contradiction at the heart of even the "struggle" to eradicate racism. Since the concept of race has informed progressive and supposedly enlightened thinking, attempts to destroy the system of racism in its primary form—Christian racism—and in derivative forms such as apartheid have been compromised from the beginning.

Until it is understood that scientifically and theologically, the notion of race when defined as a permanent or fixed division of humanity is unwarranted, population groups will be identified in thought that reifies what does not exist. Strategies for de-racisization (eradication of the concept of race from contemporary thought and behavior) that are informed by this concept will be ineffectual in such a case, no matter how radical may be the means that they employ. In other words, "race" as defined by racists does not matter because it does not exist. But racism does matter, especially in its "Christian" manifestations, because it negates entirely the churches' search for union with others in the body of Christ. Only when "race" denotes all humans, that is, the human race, is it a valid scientific and theological construct.

This awareness of how tightly Western Christianity has become ensnared in racism has led, therefore, to the contemporary "radical" (as in "rooting out") approach to eradicate racism. The emerging recognition that racism is a deeply rooted belief system, not merely an economic or colonial system of control, means that the churches must destroy racism where it has made itself most problematically at home: in Western Christianity. The problem is not that racism is simply a fringe aspect of Christianity, one embraced by persons who have not grasped the core of the gospel—though such people and groups certainly are dramatic in their racism—for that would be a fairly easy thing to disavow and root out. Rather, the racism about which we are concerned here is like the worm in the core of the apple; quietly, with no fanfare and little external sign, it has made itself at home, and the rot has spread at the very heart of Christian communities.

The foundation for an appropriate theological understanding of the meaning of all human association is this: God created the human race. The human way of expressing this unitary truth is through the formation of community—for Christians, the inherited category is koinonia (see Acts 2:42). Koinonia is a requisite of church life because it reflects the creative intent of God as well as the redemptive intent of Christ to bring all things into one. Human beings are to live in community in a way that reflects the organic union of created equals. The Hebrew Scriptures put that unitive vision in terms of its prophetic hope for the unity of the "people of God."[16] Christian imaginative language has long echoed this belief in its description of the church as the body of Christ and of individual believers and, ultimately, all human beings as imago Dei. Christians have to recognize the very complicity of the churches in misrepresentations that have legitimated the mythology of race. They must come to believe that Christians and churches are not divided by race; they are destroyed by it.

The challenge to the ecumenical minority among the churches, then, is to move beyond Christian racism by modeling a nonracial church life lived as a sign of hope in a world that is broken by so-called racial and ethnic divisions. An appropriate piety for the struggle is still the Reformation and, specifically, the Anabaptist model of resistance to tyrannical forces, in this case, the controlling force of a faith rooted in distortions of the Christian gospel. But that piety must be embodied in the personal and communal behaviors that stand against race (as a false defining construct) and racism (a false belief-faith system).

A RADICAL VISION OF THE CHURCH IN ECUMENICAL SOCIAL ETHICS

As an appropriate piety is emerging from the churches' movement into nonracial life, ecumenical social ethics is also evolving around a vision of the church rooted in "radical Reformation" social thought and practice. There has been a shift from the emphasis on social change, which moves responsible churches along the axis of love/justice, freedom, and peace norms, to a commitment to the transformation of churches and cultures now.[17]

One approach to the churches' movement into nonracial community views development as process and analyzes the movement of change in three levels.[18] From this perspective, observed patterns of adjustment, growth, and transition give clues about how radical and enduring change can be shown to take place. As the following outline indicates, three interrelated components of the change process are identified as dynamic elements in the life of the person or corporate entity (church, community, denomination, etc.) that intends radical change. The levels on which change as movement develops are information, transformation, and formation.

According to this analysis, change is primarily a function of values and relationships. That is, the process of systemic change brings together "stake-holders" whose decisions and actions result from their interactions as these are structured by the three levels of change. At the first level, information or knowledge is derived from study and experience, in this case information about the origins and effects of Christian racism. At the second level, a marked change is made in the form or appearance of an entity—it is converted, as when the churches find their deepest meaning in wholeness rather than in institutional separation. At the third level, the entity is given form or shape—it is arranged in a prescribed manner for a particular purpose and is in a process in which all of its parts are related to one another, as in nonracial koinonia community. Consider the diagram in figure 2.

NEW MODELS

The development of a beyond-Christian-racism tradition depends upon a multiple strategy approach to change in population group relations. The challenge

Figure 2. Systematic Transformation

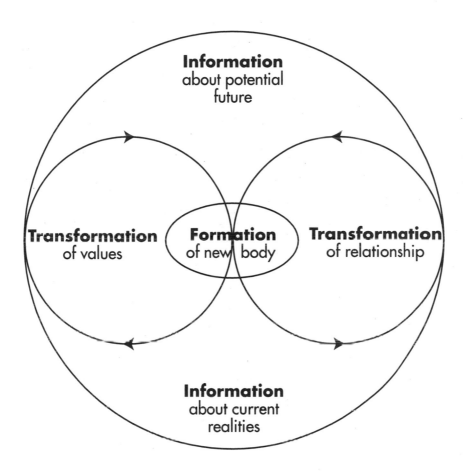

here is personal and structural change at the level of individual believers, congregations, judicatories, and other expressions of church life. These models must encompass moral policy in the churches as well as public policy making through which the churches relate to other religious traditions and to the broader community. Critical areas of thought must be challenged, and new ways of perceiving "others" must be internalized. For example, "white" and "black" must be understood as designations for social, economic, and political locations rather than as names for ontological realities.[19] "Racial" paradigms must be redone; the current paradigms must be recognized as false ways of relating to others in society.

In practical terms, people identified as "white" or of European descent must become the lead agents of the move beyond racism and the destructive category of race. They must accomplish this shift in direction, despite continuing resistance in places as diverse as South Africa, Louisiana, and western Germany, for as they are the dominant force that has maintained and disseminated the myth of race, so they must be the ones who legitimate the rejection of dominant power by participating in the dismantling of the patterns, attitudes, structures, and institutions of that illicit power.[20]

Eventually, the move beyond Christian racism must involve all the churches and individual believers, for it is only when Christians in significant numbers are engaged in moving beyond Christian racism and its concomitant elements (e.g., "white dread")[21] that we will begin to see emerging nonracial churches able to model a nonracial world. That may mean for all the churches such dramatic developments as a move beyond denominational models to a model that makes sure that all the people in a local area are being served. The New Delhi principle of local ecumenism—"all in each place" (World Council of Churches Assembly, 1961)—must become a cardinal principle of ecclesial conversion in this movement.[22]

Such nonracial modeling would relativize all cultures and culturally based social constructs. This might mean, for instance, that we would have to come to terms with the awareness that "black spirituality" does not name a reality that is biologically determined. Local communities would come to reflect the pluriform nature of the place in which they meet and whose needs they serve. If "allness" is constitutive of life in koinonia, then the churches must examine whether they should redo the patterns of association that were once considered acceptable, rooted as they are in ethnic and racial identities. Nothing short of such a radical restructuring of social patterns of association will overcome the reality that the most segregated places in the United States are still Christian churches at 11:00 A.M. on Sunday.

In the late twentieth century, churches in which repentance-action by the ecumenical minority is lived out in innovative and restorative ways model the new creation in which the gift of nonracial community is received. Authentic changes, the outcome of mission, witness that these churches are living in the midst of suffering. Discerning the way of faithful discipleship, they are transformed as they regroup around suffering rather than continuing in patterns of self-sufficiency and isolation. They live in the world, finding the concrete social meaning of the cross. Their new life embodies koinonia as old ways are transformed. They are signs of salvation, nonracial communities that are redemptive within church life and bearers of hope in the transformation mission in the world.

My purpose has been to assist in focusing the churches on our prophetic ministry of transformation, for a nonracial church in a nonracial world is the only kind of church that is congruent with the images "people of God," "body of Christ," and "household of God." The emergence of this church is cause for celebration. My hope is that the time for jubilation is near—the time when, because the whole church will be living in nonracial community, churches and world will rejoice. There will be a sacred Year of Jubilee (Lev. 25:8–19). The sounding of the trumpet will be heard throughout all lands. And all the people will be glad. Hallelujah! (See Rev. 19:1; 21:3–4.)

QUESTIONS

1.   If race does not exist as a biological reality, as Karefa-Smart argues, what other language would you use in its place? How would your actions change if you saw people of other races as people from different social backgrounds rather than races?

2.   George Kelsey's book *Racism and the Christian Understanding of Man* is referenced by several authors in this volume. How might you develop a study group to pursue the ideas presented in this chapter about the Western Christian development of racially based distinctions between people?

3.   Given the social, ethnic, and language differences in your community, how might your church begin to model a nonracial world?

4.   Karefa-Smart sees the church as an alternative society that distinguishes itself from the culture(s) in which it lives. What would happen in your congregation if it began to see itself as an alternative to the larger culture? How would your internal structures change? How would worship and service be altered? How would your relationship to the community around you change?

14 A Sharing of Gifts and Struggles in God's Will and Our Unity

JEFFREY GROS

WHEN RICHARD ALLEN WALKED OUT of St. George's Church in Philadelphia more than two centuries ago, he was making a confessional statement about the unity of God's creation and of Christ's redemption. This statement about the incompatibility of racism with faith in the triune God is central to any orthodox ecclesiology. Until the stigma of racism is eradicated from the church, it cannot be a credible witness to the world. In the U.S. context, until the historically dominant Protestant, Catholic, Orthodox, and Anglican churches have found the zeal for, and means of, restoring communion with the African American churches, the pilgrimage of the churches toward koinonia in faith, life, and witness will be without credibility.

The Faith and Order movement has made a modest contribution to the eradication of racism. In the following pages we will look briefly at (1) the history of the U.S. African American churches and the Faith and Order movement; (2) the present context in the United States as it influences the ability of the ecumenical movement and Faith and Order to contribute to the eradication of racism; and (3) proposals for a realistic future in the journey toward full visible unity in the context of the issue of racism.

Before touching these three themes, I need to lay some groundwork. The Christian churches are, by their biblical constitutions, committed to the full visible unity of the church. This is understood differently among them. For the churches of the ecumenical movement, Protestant, Catholic, Orthodox, and Anglican, this biblical commitment has been formalized for our time in the first purpose of the World Council of Churches: "to call the churches to the goal of visible unity in one faith and in one eucharistic fellowship expressed in worship and in common life in Christ, and to advance toward that unity in order that the world may believe."[1]

The quest for full visible unity entails not only reconciliation between divided churches, but also reconciliation of the elements within the churches that inhibit their witness to their internal unity as Christ intended it. As Desmond Tutu declared in his 1993 Faith and Order address, apartheid could not have developed save for the divisions within the Christian church. Unity within and between the churches may be a precondition for reconciliation. Indeed, as John Deschner notes, "Eucharistic worship must remain free to be the sacrament of unity in racial matters also, and to become the context within which we can learn afresh that when reconciliation does not imply liberation, or liberation reconciliation, both are false."[2]

The vision of visible unity, including the eradication of racism in the eucharistic heart of the Christian community, will require a deep conversion on the part of Christians and of the institutions that serve the church. Clarity of vision is an important aspect of each element of the ecumenical movement. Kortright Davis rightly observes, "Reality wrongly perceived leads inexorably to unreality strongly believed."[3] William Watley's *Singing the Lord's Song in a Strange Land*, a recent volume on the African American churches in the United States, should be an important contribution to this process.[4]

The initiative for reconciliation with the African American churches, and for the ecumenical participation of African American minorities in the other churches, may not come from African Americans themselves alone, for the most part, nor should it. Those whose predecessors caused the original alienation and profit by its continuance will have to create credibility in the African American community so that unity with them, and with the churches that are the offspring of white racism, will be possible.

However, the African American community has no concrete grounds for believing that privileged Christians and dominant churches are really committed to the full communion of the church unless, and until, such commitment is demonstrated by a conversion that entails personal behavior. One author comments on black ecumenism:

> Permeating the black ecumenical perspective is a persistent intimation that the white churches of Europe and the United States may be devoid of authentic Christianity and that the black church, as preserver of the faith, is likewise the source of ecumenical possibility. "Inclusiveness," from this perspective, is not a matter of blacks and other disinherited peoples clamoring to be admitted to the white church, but of whites being invited by blacks and others of the Two-Thirds World to return to the fold.[5]

THE AFRICAN AMERICAN CHURCHES
AND FAITH AND ORDER

From the initiation of the Faith and Order movement in Lausanne (1927), theological leaders from the U.S. African American churches were present and active. From the very beginning of the World Council of Churches (1948), Dr. Benjamin Mays sat on the Central Committee. The constitutions of Faith and Order and of the World Council and the Toronto Statement, "The Church, the Churches and the World Council of Churches," (1950) can be claimed by the African American churches as part of their heritage in the ecumenical movement.

However, the first phase of Faith and Order, 1927–52, may be considered quite nonthreatening to the identities of the white churches. The phase was characterized by a method spoken of as "comparative ecclesiology" in which the differences were noted and compared without mutual admonition or calls for change or renewal of one another. In such a context the racial origin and composition of the African American churches were noted, but did not come under scrutiny as a judgment on the churches from which they emerged. African American leaders such as Bishop William Jacob Wells remained active, but many of the African American ecumenical leaders chose minimal participation as their strategy for judgment on their ecumenical partners.

METHODOLOGICAL SHIFT: CHRISTOCENTRIC METHOD

With the 1952 World Conference a corner was turned with significant impact on Faith and Order's ability to be an appropriate instrument for eradicating ecclesiological apartheid. The first element of this change was to move from the method of comparative ecclesiology to a "Christocentric method."[6] This method focuses on the common sources of Scripture and the tradition to develop common formulations that provide both a basis for uniting the churches and a source of common renewal of the churches: "As we seek to draw closer to Christ we come closer to one another. We need, therefore, to penetrate behind our divisions to a deeper and richer understanding of the mystery of the God-given union of Christ with his church. We need increasingly to realize that the separate histories of our Churches find their full meaning only if seen in the perspective of God's dealings with his whole people."[7]

Racism as a Theological Issue

A second contribution of the Lund meeting to the eradication of racism was a revision of the Faith and Order constitution. At the Lund meeting there had been a serious discussion of social, contextual, and institutional barriers to church union. Prior to Lund these were grouped under the category of "nontheological factors." However, these factors, though different from creedal formulations, may be no less "theological" than the Reformation doctrine of justification, for example. The reworded constitution placed "relevant social, cultural, racial and other factors" squarely in the center of the theological questions of faith and order as they bear on the unity of the church.[8]

At the 1963 Montreal World Conference meeting, during the height of the U.S. civil rights struggle, William Stringfellow, an American Episcopalian, articulated the theological contradiction of racism in the sacramental understanding of the church: Baptism, he observed, is not a topic for comparative ecclesiology, but the "substantive issue in the racial crisis" in America and elsewhere. Therefore, he said, baptism is reconciliation—of all persons and all creation in the life of God.[9] This comment, and other such concerns during these early days of the sacramental discussion, enabled the final text of "Baptism, Eucharist and Ministry" (1982) to have firm statements on racism in both the baptism and the eucharist sections of the final text.

At the same Montreal Conference, the Section Report "All in Each Place" noted:

> But does the life of the Church in each place assert the dignity of the human person as God's gift?... We are shamefully divided by racial prejudice and discrimination.... In Christ there is no defense or excuse for the willful continuation of groups, church meetings or fellowships which are racially exclusive. We therefore call upon Christians in their local churches to show the marks of Christian discipleship whatever the cost.[10]

The Contextual Method

To the Christocentric method, the Louvain meeting of WCC Faith and Order (1971) added the contextual method. This method was obviously implicit in the preceding research and texts, if not always acknowledged. However, with Louvain, both the contextual influence on biblical and historical hermeneutics and the importance of attention to the present contextual reality were acknowledged.

Fifth World Conference on Faith and Order

The Santiago meeting in August 1993 reiterated the concern to keep the struggle against racism central in its "Message to the Churches":

> The deeper koinonia which is our goal is for the glory of God and for the sake of the world.... Only a church itself being healed can convincingly proclaim healing to the world. Only a church that overcomes ethnic, racial, and national hatreds in a common Christian and human identity can be a credible sign of freedom and reconciliation. While our particular focus at this conference has been the visible unity of the church, the horizon of our work has been the wider reach of God's love.[11]

The section reports also include significant notes, harvesting the work done to date on koinonia, and proposing deepening of the work of the churches as they move forward together: "All members belong but not all are the same; they are given to each other with their differences of personality, race, gender, physical abilities, social and economic status. Thus difference is not a factor to exclude anyone from the koinonia of the church, especially when such differences are expressive of weakness or vulnerability."[12] While racism, among many other church-dividing issues, has been put on the agenda, tensions remain within and between the churches in their pilgrimage toward full communion.

FAITH AND ORDER CONTRIBUTIONS FROM THE UNITED STATES

The U.S. Protestant theologians, in particular, have carried a strong initiative from the 1950s, and if one considers the contribution of H. Richard Niebuhr's *Social Sources of Denominationalism,* since the 1920s, in keeping racism before the churches. This has been an important contribution to the Orthodox, Catholic, Lutheran, and Anglican communities whose methodology has tended to be more classical and whose view of Christian divisions more historical than contextual. The conciliar movement, in its National Council and local and regional expressions, has tended to focus more on witness in the world than the unity of the church and has made a significant contribution to the quest for racial justice.[13]

U.S. Faith and Order has been especially focused on the contextual methodology in its dealings with the Community of Women and Men in the Church Study, the Contextual Theology Study, and more recently the Unity of the Church and the Renewal of Human Community Study, out of which this racism study has emerged. The Renewal of Human Community Study has been much indebted to the action/reflection methodology, which attempts to take very critical account of social location: "First, what happens when we take those who have been placed on the fringes and put their experience in the center of the theological circle? Second, what happens to our theological constructs when we raise up sociological concepts and explore how these two spheres function interdependently?"[14]

THE CONSULTATION ON CHURCH UNION

In the United States, the most mature Faith and Order proposal including African American churches is that developed in the Consultation on Church Union. COCU, as the proposal is known, proposes Covenant Communion between the Episcopal, Presbyterian, United Methodist, African Methodist Episcopal, African Methodist Episcopal Zion, Christian Methodist Episcopal Churches, the United Church of Christ, the Christian Church/Disciples of Christ, and the International Council of Community Churches.[15] These churches would incorporate into their life congregational, presbyterial, and episcopal elements of ecclesiology, provide a common vision for mission, and arrange for means of common consultation, ordination, and sacramental sharing.

The COCU text itself incorporates the concerns of the African American churches. These concerns were designated Alerts and placed in appendices in earlier drafts. The original authors of the Alerts wrote that "our deepest differences reach beyond sacraments and ministry into the divisions that tragically separate the human family." These differences "are themselves theological in that they distort God's plan to bring all creation together, everything in heaven on earth, with Christ as head (Eph. 1:10)." Where racism is concerned, the Alerts asked, "Why ought we expect to be brothers and sisters of equal status in the Church of Christ Uniting when members of the majority refuse to live next door as neighbors?"[16]

As the COCU documents elaborate on the note of common mission as essential to the united church, so justice is an inescapable element, along with evangelism and social service: "(43) It is appropriate to add something more specific regarding the church's action in mission, in view of the racial and ethnic diversity of the covenant communion. Christian unity, for churches of predominantly African American membership, is a subject never far removed from struggles to overcome poverty and to achieve social, economic, and racial justice."[17]

Obviously, the usefulness of these proposals for a Church of Christ Uniting will rest very heavily on how effective the churches have been over the last three decades in coming to know one another and forming their own people ecumenically.[18]

PRESENT ECUMENICAL SITUATION

At the present time the very vision of what the conciliar movement is called to emphasize worldwide is under question. At the Canberra Assembly (1991) the true diversity of the Christian community around the world was on display, including the appropriate prominence of the U.S. African American churches. The statement on unity approved by the Assembly, "The Unity of the Church as Koinonia: Gift and Calling," includes the commitment to "overcome divisions based on race, gender, age, culture, color and to bring all people into communion with God," and a challenge to the churches to a recommitment to justice.[19]

One of the most heated debates at Canberra was on diversity. The text now reads:

> Diversities which are rooted in theological traditions, various cultural, ethnic or historical contexts are integral to the nature of communion; yet there are limits to diversity. Diversity is illegitimate when, for instance, it makes impossible the common confession of Jesus Christ as God and Savior the same yesterday, today and forever (Heb. 13:8); salvation and the final destiny of humanity as proclaimed in Holy Scripture and preached by the apostolic community.[20]

Although the question of "illegitimate" diversity stirred deep concerns, it was quite clear that racism in the church is not a difference that can be allowed in confessing the faith preached by the apostolic community. This understanding was also made quite explicit in the Fifth World Conference on Faith and Order, in Archbishop Tutu's and other addresses, as well as in the reports of the Sections.

PROPOSALS

In 1988 the Harlem Consultation on "The Unity of the Church and the Renewal of Human Community" of the World Council, hosted by the U.S. National Council, made a series of proposals to U.S. Faith and Order, WCC Faith and Order, and the African American churches. They included the following:

1. The black churches, the United States churches and World Council leadership should support the Black Church Liaison Committee of the United States Conference of the World Council of Churches.
2. World Council leadership should explore ways of financing full participation on the part of the black churches.
3. World Council leadership should explore ways of bringing minorities, ethnic and caste groups together in participation.
4. Ecumenical leadership should take account of the contributions of black church women, especially in connection with Ecumenical Decade of the Churches in Solidarity with Women.[21]

Some of these recommendations were fulfilled in the Canberra Assembly of the World Council and the Fifth World Conference on Faith and Order, while others are under consideration, and still others have been set aside as much because of changes in the council as because of neglect.[22]

Despite the dramatic strides that have been made, the churches remain divided, and among these divisions racism remains a scandal to the Christian gospel and to the biblical doctrine of the church. Theological discussion and congregational study need to be intensified to provide their appropriate contribution to a nonracial communion of Word and Sacrament. These studies raise significant questions for scholars, church leaders, educators, and anyone who takes on the responsibility of Christ's cross in baptism.[23]

In talking about these steps that have been made to undergird God's will for the unity of the church, of the races, and of the separated churches, account must be taken of the hopeful signs we see in concrete congregations. We find within particular churches multiracial congregations who have found ways of allowing the variety of racial gifts to provide a rich service of worship and social ministry. In each of our communities examples can be cited from different Christian communions. These experiences need to be shared with other congregations to help people understand how a "postracist" community can thrive.

Ecumenical experiences of clusters of congregations, joint congregations, or common community ministries witness to the possibilities of a multiracial basis being built for a united church. The barriers of race, on occasion, can be bridged even before the barriers of confessional, sacramental, and missional life can be solved. These communities of hope, on the one hand, are served by the theological discussion of Faith and Order and, on the other, give witness to the reconciliation held before the churches themselves by these congregations.

QUESTIONS

1.   What steps are needed if the unity of Christ's church is to be served?

2.   How are African American church issues best surfaced in the ecumenical dialogue, in Christian education, and in theological training?

3.   What steps need to be taken in the local community if the unity Christ wills is to occur? What particular urgency do the divisions between churches whose origins lie in white racism present to all Christians of whatever race or communion?

4.   What do the churches need to know and to study so that the gifts of the African American churches may be celebrated by all Christians?

5.   What signs of an inclusive community do we see now that need to be nurtured?

6.   What are the priorities of the African American churches in our community? Of the churches of other racial or ethnic composition? How do we come to a common set of priorities for our ecumenical common witness?

APPENDIX:
A GUIDE TO ADDRESS RACISM
AND WORK FOR JUSTICE

INTRODUCTION
The Purpose

The purpose of this guide is to help local groups work for racial justice in their communities.[1] It has a special focus on understanding and challenging institutional racism in local communities. It also suggests ways of exploring the relationships between racism and other forms of oppression.

By institutional racism we mean the ways in which beliefs about white superiority and white social domination of the United States have been an intrinsic part of all its social structures—economic, political, educational, familial, religious, medical, communicational, and cultural life. Thus, we link expressions of individual prejudice and bigotry to larger patterns of socialization, power, and privilege—or their absence.

We have chosen this focus on purpose. This country has been uniquely founded on and much of its material wealth gained from racism—from slavery, the genocide of indigenous people, and the often forced and generally underpaid labor of many ethnic and racial groups, as well as poor white women and men. In many parts of the country that have small populations of people of color, it is easy to forget some of this history and to pretend that racism does not exist in a specific location or that it is expressed only in a specific bigoted remark or assault. But racism is an intrinsic part of the U.S. reality, wherever we live, and if we are to move toward a genuinely just future, racism must be understood and challenged, along with patriarchy, heterosexism, classism, ageism, ableism, and the violence done to the earth.

This guide looks primarily at white racism toward African Americans. It could be adapted for other expressions of racism, but with caution. It is important to be specific. The history of white interaction with other peoples—Native Americans, Asians and Asian Americans, Mexican Americans, for instance—is a different history from that of white interaction with African Americans. Some of the dynamics and issues are different. For many Native Americans, justice demands self-government and a land base. Justice for African Americans involves redistributing institutional power and access to resources. The changes are equally fundamental, but do not necessarily include an autonomous political and cultural/spiritual structure.

This focus does not mean that only whites and blacks can participate in these sessions, of course. We encourage you to create as racially diverse a group as is possible in your area. It can also be a white-only group.

This guide, therefore, is designed to help groups understand the presence of racism in society and in our lives: its relation to other forms of oppression and ways of overcoming it. It seeks to engage groups in a process for determining what they can do right where they live to join in the global struggle for justice.

The guide includes a six-session outline of questions and exercises with some written and visual resources. Each session is designed to last two hours. In the last session, the group will be asked to decide if it wishes to stay together for further exploration of the presence of racism as well as to determine specific actions.

The group for which this is written can be a new group or one of which you are already a member. If it is new, invite people to commit at least six weeks for exploration, consciousness raising, social analysis, and planning.

The Process

Although no extensive or expert knowledge about racism in the United States is necessary to facilitate the following sessions, some basic awareness is desirable. Similarly, the leader does not have to be an expert on group process. To make this guide as accessible as possible, detailed instructions and descriptions are given for each session. They may be much too detailed for leaders and groups with experience in these areas; please feel free to modify what is given in any way that makes sense to you.

As leader, you are more of a facilitator than instructor, and two of you may wish to facilitate together. If it is at all possible, a team of two people of differing racial or ethnic heritage will provide the most effective leadership.

We suggest that you read through the entire guide carefully and keep in mind the flow of one session with the next. Think about the questions, process, and suggestions in each session, and adapt them to your situation. Try to set an atmosphere in which people can speak honestly without fear of criticism. Encourage people to use "I" statements, to express "what I think or feel" or what "my experience has been."

SESSION 1

Purpose: to introduce the group to the sessions and to begin the examination of racism in their lives.

I. Introduction

Begin by asking participants to introduce themselves and to describe briefly why they are here and what they hope to gain from the six sessions.

Then give members an overview of the sessions: times, dates, and any other business matters.

II. Showing the Video

Show a video that examines the history of African Americans in your particular region. Such videos are available at rental stores, through your public library, denominational offices, or university libraries. If none are available, you might show a video on the more general experience of African Americans or invite person(s) to share their stories. Several videos are listed in the bibliography.[2]

After the video, ask for any responses of members, and then begin a discussion.

What did you know about black history in your area before you saw the film? Where did you learn it, or more likely, why did you not learn it? What do you know of your own ethnic/racial history?

For people whose story has been suppressed, learning that story becomes a significant source of identity, pride, and power. It provides resources for continuing the struggle for freedom and dignity. For those of us who are white and already engaged in anti-racism work, it is sometimes difficult to find similar resources. Ask each person to identify dimensions of her or his history that offer positive resources for identity, power, and direction in the struggle for justice.

Conclude by asking each one to identify something positive from the session and any suggestion to improve the next one. These are not for discussion but for each one to take responsibility for what happens as well as to affirm and help the facilitators in planning. Assure people that they can pass if they wish to.

SESSION 2

Purposes: (*a*) to help people identify feelings about themselves as members of certain cultural or racial groups; (*b*) to identify some of their feelings about working with people of different racial/cultural groups; and (*c*) to begin examining the interrelations of different patterns of oppression in this society.

It is very important that people feel comfortable enough to share uncomfortable feelings and insights and at the same time not to feel pressured to share more than they are willing to. You may want to begin with a discussion of ground rules for this and other sessions. Ask participants to formulate the rules they wish to operate by (e.g., no one's sharing goes beyond this room; no one is to be pushed to share beyond what she or he volunteers; all feelings and experiences are authentic and to be respected). Post them where they can be seen during each session and call members' attention to them if they seem to forget them.

I. Exploring Our Cultural/Racial Identities

If the group is large, subdivide into small groups of three or four. Ask if people prefer groups composed of the same racial backgrounds, e.g., all black, white, etc. (Same-race groups may be very important if people do not know one another well and/or trust one another.)

A. Ask the members of each group to name one characteristic, activity, adjective, or event typically related to the group of which she or he is proud and then one of which she or he is ashamed or by which she or he is hurt.

B. Ask members of each group to name what it means to each one to be a member of their race and when and how they became significantly aware that they were in fact African American or European American or Hispanic American or Asian American, etc. Remind people to focus just on racial membership (if people are biracial, ask them what groups they have been put into by "society" as well as the significance of an identity that is not simply black, white, etc.).

C. Ask each group to formulate two statements about themselves they would most like African Americans to hear.

Ask the groups to determine why those particular statements are important. For instance, what fears, hopes, anxieties, and/or struggles do they reflect? Also, ask the white group to explore the extent to which members want honest answers.

Ask any groups or individuals of color to explore the risks, limits, and commitments for themselves to honest communication with whites in general and with those here.

II. We Are Members of Many Social Groups

Now, point out that we belong to several groups, perhaps with quite different histories. One person may be black and female and straight; another white, male, and gay; still another male, white, but French in a Yankee-dominated town.

A. Ask people to pair off, and each one to identify those different relationships in their lives. (If there are gay and lesbian people present, some may be reluctant to name their identification in those groups. Acknowledge that reluctance and assure people that you are not asking them to identify themselves in ways that they do not feel comfortable.)

Ask each partner in turn to name one characteristic, activity, adjective, or event typically related to the groups she or he is a member of that she or he is proud of and then ashamed of or hurt by. Each person should take at least ten minutes, while her or his partner listens and, without making any judgment, encourages the other to be as specific as possible. Then ask each to identify and share with the other tensions, conflicts, and/or harmonies that she or he experiences from membership in those multiple groups.

B. Finally, ask the pairs to come together in a large circle and choose one thing to share with the whole group.

C. You might close with an exercise similar to the one in Session 1.

SESSION 3

Purpose: this session and the next explore institutional racism in more depth.

A. Hand out the definitions of racism, stereotyping, etc., found in the introduction to this volume. Ask people to read them, and then in the large group, ask for their examples of each concept. This is an opportunity for clarification and for making abstract concepts concrete.

B. Then introduce what follows with something like this: "Since racism (and other forms of oppression) can be understood by examining institutional or social power, cultural beliefs, unearned privilege, access to resources, stereotyping, and the threat and use of violence, we will look at each of these in more detail. We will examine three of these each session."

I. Social Power

A. Ask each one to write down answers to the following: First, identify a social role you play that is important to you. A social role is a role in an institution (e.g., a teacher or a student or a principal in a school; a wife, a partner in a family; an employee in a business; a volunteer in a social change organization; a member of a religious community). Then, describe the social power you have in that role (What do you have the power to do? Are you autonomous or accountable to others? Do your responsibilities and your authority seem equal? Compared to other roles in the institution, is yours one of significant power?). To what extent is it exercised in a hierarchical structure (i.e., in a pattern in which power flows down from the top and people on each level below are accountable to those above)? As you think about the various areas of your life—jobs or other economic areas (e.g., welfare), professional life, family, politics, religious communities, cultural contexts, education, health, volunteer organizations—how would you rate the degree of social power you have?

In small groups, spend about ten minutes sharing conclusions. Then ask the groups to explore where in those institutions, if at all, different racial groups are congregated or whether they are equally distributed throughout the hierarchy. Why do you think the pattern exists as it is? Has it, for instance, been different in the past? Is it likely to be different in the future? What keeps the pattern in place? What inhibits change?

B. Ask someone (this could be done in advance of this session) to describe what it is like being "the only one" (or one of a few, a token) of a racial group, if possible, or of some other group, if not (the only woman, the only gay person, the only person over fifty) in a social institution, e.g., a school or class, a job or level of management, etc. If there are enough people with this kind of experience, there could be one for each small group. Otherwise, ask one or two persons to share with the whole group. Then, in small groups, ask members to share what it's like being one of many—working, learning, etc., both in a context in which some people have more power than others and also being one with others who have equal power, e.g., as a white student in a school that is 98 percent white.

II. Access to Resources

Now, ask the group to examine how access to resources functions and how it is related to social power. You might begin by saying that one of the functions of an institution is to distribute the resources and rewards of a society to its members—food, for instance, or money or status in the community or power.

A. In small groups, identify some of the resources and rewards of the institution you are working with. What are the resources—material, social, and psychological—and rewards of the institution you are examining (e.g., good grades, necessary for a good job; promotion, higher pay, etc.)?

Follow that with such questions as these (you might put them on newsprint so each group can address them at its own pace):

- Who is/are the gatekeeper(s) to those resources and rewards? (Who determines who gets access to the resources and rewards and on what basis?)
- Has there been/is there now in that institution any consensus among different races about who has access to resources and rewards and on what basis?
- Where do standards of excellence or other qualifications come from? How is access to resources and rewards related to race, to social power in that institution?

B. Ask members to return to the definition of racism and draw their own conclusions about the extent of racism in their community. What now does that mean to them?

III. Cultural Beliefs

Institutional racism is supported and justified by an ethos, a pattern of beliefs and values that to some extent everyone in this society is socialized into whether she or he is white or not. This pattern determines what is true, right, normative. For instance, white skin is normative; black is "other." The norm for female beauty is still a certain combination of whiteness, youth, slimness, and curves. African Americans who most closely fit this pattern are more likely to be included in the category of beautiful than those with other features. It is much more acceptable to the dominant culture for whites to adopt a child of color than the reverse. European American heritage shapes educational curricula from kindergarten to graduate school. It is considered much more important to know about the Italian Renaissance than the Harlem Renaissance. Such assumptions are pervasive. They are part of the cultural air we all breathe.

A. Ask the group to brainstorm other cultural truths and values. Ask them to identify two kinds of beliefs and values: (1) those related directly to white/European heritage superiority (like the ones listed above) and (2) other beliefs that have been central to the dominant culture, such as the belief that the nuclear heterosexual family is normative, the belief that income should be dependent on jobs, and many beliefs about what it means to be a woman or a man in this culture.

B. After a list has been generated, ask the group to form small groups and explore:

1. The connections between the two lists, e.g., how does the belief about the normativeness of the nuclear family reinforce beliefs about white superiority or the belief that income should depend on jobs?

2. How such beliefs and values reinforce and/or challenge the patterns of social power and access to resources.

C. Group members will probably find this session quite depressing. You may wish to conclude with asking each one to identify briefly another belief or value in her or his heritage that challenges racism. If people of color are present, ask them if they can identify a belief or value in the white/European heritage that challenges racism.

D. Ask each one to share an insight or something else positive from the session and any suggestion for improvement for the next session.

SESSION 4

Purpose: this session continues the exploration of institutional racism as we examine stereotyping, unearned white privilege, and violence.

I. Stereotyping

Begin by asking members in the large group to name some stereotypes of African Americans or people of other ethnic/racial groups held by white people in this country. List them on newsprint.

Then ask the group to break into small groups and explore such questions as the following: Where do you think they come from? How are they perpetuated, passed down from generation to generation? What institutions in this society help communicate ideas and values? What role do you see that they play in communicating stereotypes? How do stereotypes regulate access to resources and re-wards? How do you think they legitimate maintaining power in the hands of whites? To what extent do you think it is easier/harder to stereotype people when there are none, only one, or a few in an institutional context (e.g., a school) or in a majority? Why?

II. Unearned White Privilege

Following this discussion of stereotyping, introduce the concept of unearned white privilege (i.e., power, statuses, freedoms that you have because you are white). You might summarize Peggy McIntosh's article.[3] List some of the ex-amples she identified of white privilege in her life.

A. Ask each white person to write down at least five examples of unearned white privilege in his or her life. If people from other ethnic/racial groups are present, ask them to list five examples of white privilege they experience from white people.

B. Ask people to share and ask them how difficult they found the exercise to be. It is likely that they found it difficult. Ask people what it feels like to them to have privilege that they did not earn and that others do not have. Point out that unearned privilege is related to social power. It is a reward for being white in this society. Ask people how this racially based allocation of privilege helps to main-tain oppression.

C. Ask people to form pairs and examine at least two other cultural/racial groups they identified in Session 2 that they are members of. How do the dimen-sions of social power, generous or limited access to resources, and unearned privilege exist for them in each of the groups they have identified? Where, if at all, are there conflicts? How might you use your access or lack of access to those real-ities to work for justice?

III. Violence

Finally, suggest to the group that you will look at violence and how it expresses and helps to maintain racism. Ask people to pair off again, giving people the op-tion of same-race pairs. Ask each in turn to name some of the ways in which people of specific cultural/racial groups are hurt by the patterns you have been talking about (racially based social power, access to resources and rewards, un-earned privilege, and stereotyping). Identify emotional, physical, and spiritual violence.

Then ask the pairs to identify ways in which whites are harmed by this pat-tern. How is the harm similar, and how is it different? How might you name those differences? What adjectives, for instance, might you use? Someone has sug-gested, for instance, that blacks are oppressed and whites are dehumanized.

IV. Conclusion

Conclude this session with preparation for research in the community to answer such questions as: What is happening in this community to address racism? Are there areas of particular tension or conflict?

Ask the group to list areas they would like to explore (e.g., local schools, police, shelters, businesses). Perhaps a couple of people could be responsible for each area selected. Then brainstorm the questions to ask of each area (What racial diversity exists? How racially based is power? What is communicated implicitly/explicitly about whites and people of other cultural/racial groups? How welcome would people of color be? What role do people of color play in determining how the resources and rewards of the area are distributed? What workshops or programs exist to train people to address racism and other forms of oppression in these areas?).

SESSION 5

Purpose: to envision what a racially just society looks like to your group and to report on the research done between this session and the last.

Introduce this session by telling the group that you are going to lead them in a guided visualization of a racially just society. What would [*this town*] look like if it had overcome racism? Participants should also include other forms of justice in their vision as they are knowledgeable: gender, sexual, class, age, abilities, etc.

I. Envisioning

Ask the group to get comfortable and relax; put concerns and responsibilities aside for the time being. Use any simple relaxation exercise you are familiar with. Now guide them into a just future. The following comments are suggestions; feel free to compose your own visualization. The pauses are important. Don't rush!

You are going on a trip into the year 2050 to visit [*town's or city's name*] as a model of racial justice. You are going to travel on a pink cloud that is large and comfortable. (Pause for 15 seconds.)

You are sitting outside watching the sun come up, and a large, soft cloud drifts down to you. You climb on. (Pause for 15 seconds.)

The cloud carries you over fields (pause for 10 seconds), trees (pause for 10 seconds), towns (pause for 10 seconds), rivers (pause for 10 seconds). You see sheep and cattle (pause for 10 seconds), ships (pause for 10 seconds), cars (pause for 10 seconds).

The cloud carefully descends toward a community that looks something like [*this one*]. (Pause for 15 seconds.)

It settles near the center of the town and you get off. (Pause for 10 seconds.)

A person comes up to you and says, "I am your guide. My name is _____." (Pause for 15 seconds.) You greet each other and off you go on a tour. (Pause for 15 seconds.)

You go to a school—to a place where kids and adults are together reading, doing carpentry, planting vegetables, working with computers. (Pause for 10 seconds.) Who belongs here? Who is welcome? (Pause for 15 seconds.)

You look at the books around you. What do you see? (Pause for 30 seconds.)

You look at the interaction of the people. What do you see? (Pause for 30 seconds.)

You ask your host, "Why do people go to school? What do they hope to get from it? What are the rewards the school makes available? Who determines the rewards and who gets them?" How does your host respond? (Pause for 30 seconds.)

Next your host takes you to a local business. What kind of business is it? What do you see? (Pause for 30 seconds.)

Again, who belongs there? Who is welcome there? How can you tell? (Pause for 30 seconds.)

Who has power in this business? What kind of power? (Pause for 30 seconds.)

You go to another workplace. Does this one look like the first one? How is it different or similar and why? (Pause for 30 seconds.)

How are workers rewarded or compensated for their work in either business? (Pause for 10 seconds.) How are the products or services made available to the rest of the community? (Pause for 30 seconds.)

As you travel with your host, you notice the homes and ask, "Is there a poor section—or a rich section?" How does your host respond and why? (Pause for 30 seconds.)

You would like to continue, but you see your cloud hovering over a public park and you know that you must leave. You thank your host and say goodbye; you climb onto the cloud. Softly, the cloud carries you back over fields and rivers and woods, over sheep and cattle, ships and cars (pause for 10 seconds) and brings you safely home. (Pause for 30 seconds.)

Now return to the present. (Pause for 60 seconds.)

Give them a minute and then ask for sharing. What did they see? You might write on newsprint key phrases, images, and nouns of their visions. After the sharing, ask the group to identify where the different or even conflicting visions are. These do not need to be resolved, simply identified, but it is important to determine whether the differences come from people of different racial identities. Ask the group how they would address these differences if they were on a town planning committee and those differences surfaced. (This is not the place to resolve them, but the group can spend a few minutes thinking about process in light of previous discussions about power and who makes decisions.)

II. Reports

Now ask for reports from the research. If there is not time for all, decide now how many to hear and plan to do the others next time. As each report is made, if there is time, you might ask how similar or different is the picture of the school (or whatever institution) in the report from the visions.

Again, conclude with appropriate sharing.

SESSION 6

Purposes: (*a*) to finish reports, if any were left over; (*b*) to decide on a course of action; and (*c*) to decide how that action will be sustained.

I. Ask for Any Outstanding Reports

II. Ask the Group What They Want to Do

Allow a few minutes for general reaction to the reports and what they indicate about what is going on in this community to address issues of racism. Then suggest they set some achievable goals. You may want to ask them to list six and then have a show of hands for how many are interested in each one and choose the top one or two. Or you may ask them to agree on one or two. The reports may have already helped engender an emerging consensus.

III. Develop Specific Changes

Once one or two goals have been set, ask what concrete, specific changes would most likely achieve or reflect those goals (e.g., ten new books in the school library that tell parts of African American history, Hispanic kids in the school becoming part of a process to determine how to make the school belong to them as well as the white kids).

IV. Focus on Particular Changes

Then decide how those changes are going to come about and who is going to do what. Some questions to keep in mind: What coalitions should/can be formed? How can we support people who are already "in the system" rather than just challenge it "from the outside"?

V. Establish a Timetable

Decide on a timetable and a process for communication/meeting throughout the course of the actions.

VI. Finish Any Other Business

Invite discussion about unfinished business within the group—issues, interests that emerged that the group may wish to explore further. It may wish to continue its own educational process, for instance, to go more in depth about racism, Native American or African American history, culture and contemporary struggles. It may wish to examine another form of oppression in depth and relate that to the struggle for racial justice. It may wish to become a support group for those working toward racial justice. It may wish to focus on building relationships of solidarity and alliance with group/organizations/individuals of color in the region. There are both a wealth of possibilities and a wealth of resources for any of these possibilities.

VII. Bring the Process to Closure

Bring these six sessions to a close in some manner appropriate to the group. Each participant, for instance, might use a phrase or image that communicates what the work together has meant for her or him. Each one might mention a phrase or image of hope for the future. A prayer or song or poem could be used to facilitate a transition from ending one process and beginning another.

NOTES

INTRODUCTION: WHAT IS RACISM?

1. Burton Tan, "A Long Time Framed and Culturally Topographically Designed Terminology—People of Color," unpublished manuscript, 1991, 3–4.

1. CASE STUDY: MINNESOTA CHURCHES' ANTI-RACISM INITIATIVE

1. *Merriam-Webster's Third New International Dictionary, Unabridged,* ed. Philip Babcock Gove (Springfield, Mass.: Merriam-Webster, 1993).

2. Barndt's elaboration, briefly summarized here, is the framework for extensive discussion during intensive seminars presented by Crossroads Ministry, Chicago, Illinois, replicated in the Minnesota Churches' Anti-Racism Initiative. The definition is quoted from a seminar handout, "Defining Race and Power."

3. Ibid.

4. Ibid.

5. Summarized from seminar handout, "Principles of Organizing to Dismantle Institutional Racism."

6. Danny Duncan Collum, "Fascism with a Facelift," in *America's Original Sin: A Study Guide on White Racism* (Washington, D.C.: Sojourners, 1992).

7. The board's decision was ratified by mail ballot in June following affirmation at a May 7 board meeting, complying with a constitutional requirement for two votes in order to change the by-laws, as needed to create a new program. An anti-racism workshop followed the May 7 meeting.

8. The Minnesota Churches' Anti-Racism Initiative has been led since mid-1995 by James and Nadine Addington, codirectors of the Tri-Council Coordinating Commission.

3. COLOR LINES AND THE RELIGION OF RACISM

1. It was ironic that W. E. B. DuBois succumbed on the eve of the August 1963 March on Washington when Martin Luther King Jr. delivered his famous "I Have a Dream" speech.

2. The late Professor George Kelsey, former ethicist at Drew Theological Seminary, has written the best analysis of racism I have read. See his *Racism and the Christian Understanding of Man* (New York: Charles Scribner's Sons, 1965), esp. 146; see also Waldo Beach, "A Theological Analysis of Race Relations," in *Faith and Ethics,* ed. Paul Ramsey (New York: Charles Scribner & Sons, 1957), 211.

3. The late seminal African American preacher, theologian, philosopher, and poet Dr. Howard Thurman contributed significantly to the search for common ground. The title of his now famous book *The Search for Common Ground* became the rallying point for integrationists who needed a raison d'être in their struggle against the demonizing effects of racism. A more penetrating analysis of segregation can be found in his *Luminous Darkness*. I now cherish with great pride the rare moments of having sat at the feet of Howard Thurman during my student days in the activist sixties at Morehouse College and later during the sunset of his life in the late seventies in San Francisco.

4. COMBATING RACISM IN CHURCH AND SEMINARY

1. Peggy McIntosh, "White Privilege and Male Privilege: A Personal Account of Coming to See Correspondence through Work in Women's Studies," in *Race, Class, and Gender: An Anthology*, ed. Margaret L. Andersen and Patricia Hill Collins (Belmont, Calif.: Wadsworth, 1992).

2. Ibid., 74.

3. Ibid., 75.

4. Stephen Brookfield, *Developing Critical Thinkers: Challenging Adults to Explore Alternative Ways of Thinking and Acting* (San Francisco: Jossey-Bass, 1987).

5. William B. Kennedy, "Integrating Personal and Social Ideologies," in *Fostering Critical Reflection in Adulthood: A Guide to Transformative and Emancipatory Learning*, ed. Jack Mezirow and Associates (San Francisco: Jossey-Bass, 1990).

6. Peter Berger and Thomas Luckman, *The Social Construction of Reality* (New York: Anchor Books, 1967).

7. Thomas Groome, *Christian Religious Education: Sharing Our Story and Vision* (San Francisco: Harper & Row, 1981).

6. QUESTIONS OF INCLUSION IN THE CHRISTIAN SCRIPTURES

1. Peter J. Paris, "Race Relations after Thirty Years: In the Face of Despair," *Christian Century*, April 27, 1994, 439. See also Cornel West, *Race Matters* (Boston: Beacon Press, 1993).

2. See Mark Horst, "The Unfinished Agenda of the Civil Rights Movement," *Christian Century*, April 27, 1994, 446–48.

3. In his confession, Peter seems to have understood Jesus as a traditional Messiah, one who would apply God's power against Israel's overlord, Rome. Jesus' treatment of his suffering causes Peter to object, and Jesus identifies him with Satan, the prince of the world and the origin of its values. (See Mark 8:27–33.)

4. Author's translation here and throughout chapter.

5. Ahn Byung-Mu has the very powerful article "Jesus and the Minjung in the Gospel of Mark," in *Voices from the Margin: Interpreting the Bible in the Third World*, ed. R. S. Sugirtharajah (London: SPCK, 1991). Byung-Mu gives special attention to the social character of Jesus' audience, analyzing Mark's use of the term "crowd/s" (102).

6. Matthew calls for a righteousness greater than that of the scribes and Pharisees, perfection as God is perfect (Matt. 5:17, 48) involving even control of the inner dynamics of lust and anger. Thus, Matthew tightly draws the boundaries of righteousness and therefore inclusion/exclusion.

7. See Maurice Friedman's comments about the Buber-Rosenzweig translation in *Encounter on the Narrow Ridge: A Life of Martin Buber* (New York: Paragon House, 1993), 169.

7. ENDING RACISM IN SOCIETY THROUGH THE CHURCHES

1. Howard Thurman, *Luminous Darkness: A Personal Interpretation of the Anatomy of Segregation and the Ground of Hope* (New York: Harper & Row, 1965), 93–94.

2. Howard Thurman, *With Head and Heart* (New York: Harcourt Brace Jovanovich, 1979), 45.

3. Ibid., 46.

4. Thurman, *Luminous Darkness*, 89–90.

5. Ibid., 90.

6. Ibid., 98.

7. Howard Thurman, *The Search for Common Ground: An Inquiry into the Basis of Man's Experience of Community* (New York: Harper & Row, 1971), 28.

8. Ibid., 32.

9. Howard Thurman, *Footprints of a Dream: The Story of the Church for the Fellowship of All Peoples* (New York: Harper & Row, 1959), 29.

10. Howard Thurman, ed., *The First Footprints: The Dawn of the Idea of the Church for the Fellowship of All Peoples: Letters between Alfred Fisk and Howard Thurman, 1943–1944* (San Francisco: Lawton and Alfred Kennedy, 1975), 2.

11. Thurman, *With Head and Heart*, 33.

12. Thurman, *Footprints of a Dream*, 21.

13. Ibid.

14. Howard Thurman, "Man and the Experience of Community," unpublished essay, March 20, 1969.

15. Ibid., 1.

16. Thurman, *Footprints of a Dream*, 51. See also Alton B. Pollard III, *Mysticism and Social Change: The Social Witness of Howard Thurman* (New York: Peter Lang, 1992), 80.

17. See Thurman, *Footprints of a Dream*, 34; see also Pollard, *Mysticism*, 79.

18. Thurman, *Luminous Darkness*, 93.

8. BAPTISM AS SACRAMENT OF STRUGGLE AND RITE OF RESISTANCE

1. The title of this chapter was inspired by a discussion of black theology and ecclesiology in James H. Evans's *We Have Been Believers* (Minneapolis: Augsburg Fortress, 1992), chap. 6, "The Community of Faith and Spirit of Freedom," 119–40. Evans cites the writing of Albert Cleage and the idea that the church must be "the nation of God," an agent

of liberation in the world (132). Particularly important for this chapter is Cleage's notion of baptism as "not an escape from the world but an immersion into it" (133).

2. What is meant when I speak of baptism as a "fundamental response of discipleship" is both declarative and constitutive of the Christian faith. Again, Evans is most helpful in articulating the historic debate simply, yet not simplistically. Evans writes, "The heart of any Christian community is what it believes and practices in relation to baptism and the Lord's Supper, or the Eucharist. Through the act of baptism membership in the community of faith is confirmed" (ibid., 139).

3. Seeking the "visible unity" of the church has been the stated goal of the world ecumenical movement for more than fifty years. It is toward visible unity that this chapter reaches in taking up the problem of racism in the body of Christ. The decision of the World Alliance of Reformed Churches (WARC) to name apartheid a heresy is one particularly potent example of the lengths to which Christians must be committed to go to re-unite or re-member the body of Christ.

4. *Introductory Guide to A Brief Statement of Faith,* Presbyterian Church (U.S.A.) (Office of the General Assembly, 1990).

5. *The Recovery of Black Presence: An Interdisciplinary Exploration,* edited by Randall C. Bailey and Jacquelyn Grant (Nashville: Abingdon, 1995), explores the ways ideology and hermeneutics have impacted biblical interpretation, theology, and ethics over time. Katie G. Cannon's essay in this work, "Slave Ideology and Biblical Interpretation," cites the example of slavery and the use of the Bible to argue the importance of understanding the connection between ideology and hermeneutics (biblical/historical/ethical/theological interpretation). The distorted use of the Bible was commonplace for slave holders to maintain their control within slave society.

6. See David T. Shannon and Gayraud S. Wilmore, eds., *Black Witness to the Apostolic Faith* (Grand Rapids: Eerdmans, 1988), 10.

7. The term "God service" has been the subject of discussion in other articles written as part of the ongoing study of the theology and practice of ordination by the Presbyterian Church (U.S.A.). See "A Proposal for Considering the Theology and Practice of Ordination in the Presbyterian Church (U.S.A.)," Theology and Worship Ministry Unit, 1992.

8. See Groupe des Dombes, *For the Conversion of the Churches* (Geneva: WCC Publications, 1993). Their concept of Christian identity fits well with the image of God service that is embraced within the study document mentioned in the previous note. They write, "Christian identity is not only dialogue or relationship, it is also service, diakonia. Its primary point of reference is the Servant Christ—he who washed the feet of his disciples. Christian identity is operative in acts of service" (20).

9. One of the most glaring examples of the role race plays as both a church-dividing and a church-uniting issue remains the case of South Africa. See, for example, *Apartheid Is a Heresy,* ed. John De Gruchy and Charles Villavincencio (Grand Rapids, Mich.: Eerdmans, 1983). The story of denial and the covering up of racism as both a church-dividing and a church-uniting issue in North America is yet another sad example of what some have called the churches' failure to be the church. Will Campbell, once director of the famed Committee of Southern Churchmen and advisor to the National Council of

Churches, authored a little book a generation ago called *Race and the Renewal of the Church,* in which he cautioned whites and blacks to reckon with the seeds of racism being planted in the body of Christ.

10. See chapters 13 and 14 of this book.

11. From "In Christ There Is No East or West," by John Oxenham, 1908, altered.

9. THE EUCHARIST AND RACISM

1. Charles Murray and Richard Herrnstein, *The Bell Curve* (New York: Free Press, 1996).

2. Sharon Begley, "Three Is Not Enough," *Newsweek,* February 13, 1995, 67.

10. VIOLENCE IN THE HOUSEHOLD

1. Adrian van Kaam, *Formative Spirituality* series, vol. 1, *Fundamental Formation* (New York: Crossroad, 1983), 158.

2. Derrick Bell, *Faces at the Bottom of the Well: The Permanence of Racism* (New York: Harper Collins Basic Books, 1992), xii.

3. For more detailed material on the communal dispositions see Adrian van Kaam and Susan Muto, *Commitment: Key to Christian Maturity* (Mahwah, N.J.: Paulist Press, 1989); *The Power of Appreciation* (New York: Crossroad, 1993).

4. Van Kaam, *Fundamental Formation,* 157.

5. Ibid.

6. Adrian van Kaam, *Formative Spirituality* series, vol. 2, *Human Formation* (New York: Crossroad, 1985), 1.

7. Ibid., 10.

8. Ibid., 25–26.

9. Adrian van Kaam, *Formative Spirituality* series, vol. 5, *Traditional Formation* (New York: Crossroad, 1992), 133.

10. Van Kaam, *Human Formation,* 157.

11. Flannery O'Connor, *A Good Man Is Hard to Find* (Garden City, N.Y.: Doubleday Image, 1970), 28.

12. CONVERSION, COVENANT, COMMITMENT, AND CHANGE

1. Cornel West, *Prophetic Fragments* (Grand Rapids, Mich.: Eerdmans, 1988), 161.

2. *Christian Century,* February 24, 1993, 200.

3. Larry Rasmussen, "National Fault Lines: Is South Central L.A. a Defining Moment in a Defining Place?" (speech to the Ohio Council of Churches, December 4, 1992), 7.

4. Cited from Ans van der Bent, "The Concept of Conversion in the Ecumenical Movement," *Ecumenical Review,* October 1992, 385.

5. West, *Prophetic Fragments,* 120–21.

6. Cited in *The Montana Association of Churches' Messenger,* February 1993, 7.

13. A CALL TO MOVE BEYOND THE HERITAGE OF CHRISTIAN RACISM

1. Ans van der Bent, *Commitment to God's World: A Concise Critical Survey of Ecumenical Social Thought* (Geneva: World Council of Churches Publications, 1995), Part XI. A short bibliography of references on racism appears on p. 227.

2. Dr. Visser t'Hooft outlined this position in the "Address to the World Council of Churches-Sponsored World Consultation on Racism" held at Notting Hill, London, in 1969. He further developed his thinking about violent revolutionary change in *Has the Ecumenical Movement a Future?* (Belfast: Christian Journals, 1974), 89–90.

3. Van der Bent, *Commitment to God's World,* Parts I and II.

4. Ibid., 140.

5. Elizabeth Adler, *A Small Beginning: An Assessment of the First Five Years of the Programme to Combat Racism* (Geneva: World Council of Churches Publications, 1974).

6. *Central Committee of the World Council of Churches (WCC) Minutes and Reports of the 23rd Meeting, Canterbury, Great Britain, 1969* (Geneva: World Council of Churches Publications, 1969), Agenda Item 17, pp. 30–31. Appendix III, pp. 86–102.

7. For some of its critics, PCR went too far in its support of violent revolutionary change; resourcing the humanitarian needs of liberation movements was seen as indirect support for the military budgets of armed struggles in which the liberation movements were engaged. Other critics opposed PCR's operational guidelines, which were based on the conviction that the de-racization of churches and societies required white leadership since the voluntary transfer of economic, political, and social power was a major aim of PCR. Partnership was to be the mode of relationships between those responsible for eliminating racism from the churches—white leaders—and those who were to be the "voice" of the communities of the racially oppressed—minority leaders.

8. Baldwin Sjollentha, "Programme to Combat Racism," *Directory of the Ecumenical Movement* (Geneva: World Council of Churches Publications, 1951).

9. George D. Kelsey, *Racism and the Christian Understanding of Man* (New York: Charles Scribner's Sons, 1965), 26–35. This chapter follows closely Professor Kelsey's discussion of racism as both pseudofaith and pseudoscience.

10. Ibid., 21.

11. Ibid., introduction.

12. Ibid., 22.

13. Ibid., 23–24.

14. David Hume, for instance, spoke of the "inferiority of negroes . . . to the whites" (cited in Alan Davies, "The Ideology of Racism," in *Concilium: The Church and Racism,* ed. Gregory Baum and John Coleman [New York: Seabury Press, 1982], 15).

15. Kelsey, *Racism,* 28.

16. The "chosen people" who came to form the nation of Israel identified themselves first as the *qahal YHWH,* the "people of God," but the prophets extended that covenant consciousness to embrace the whole world, as in Isaiah's vision of universal peace founded on the "knowledge of God" (Isa. 11:9) and the dream of a covenant meal celebrated by all nations on God's holy mountain (Isa. 25:6–10).

17. They move into a transformative mode of radical change only as they discover the way to express, in new community now, the radical vision of equality, justice, and freedom. Pounded by the force of prophetic judgments (such as those expressed in some liberationist theological approaches), they struggle at many levels of expression (parish, middle judicatory, regional, and global) to move from remorse through forgiveness and restitution into structures and relations that are the fruits of restoration and reconciliation. As a result, the churches that succeed in moving into nonracial life in koinonia community are transformed in ways that are visible and new.

18. William Smith, ODII (Organizing for Development International). See chapter by Turid Sato and William Smith, "The New Development Paradigm: Organizing for Implementation," in *Development, New Paradigms and Principles for the Twentieth Century,* ed. Jo Marie Griesgreber and Bernhard G. Gunter (London: Pluto Press, 1996), 89–102.

19. Andrew Hacker, *Two Nations, Black and White, Separate, Hostile, Unequal* (New York: Scribner's, 1992).

20. There is one moral act that has been proposed during this, the third period of the ecumenical effort, to move beyond Christian racism into nonracial koinonia community. Although it is controversial and even unpopular, black reparations in my view is the only strategy on record that has the essentials for moving formerly racist churches through systemic, radical change into true koinonia communities.

"Black reparations" references an initiative in the United States, undertaken in 1969 by James Forman and the National Black Economic Conference. Their manifesto was presented to churches and synagogues. Although the literature on reparations is extensive, covering a broad range of cases, e.g., payment of indemnity to German victims of Nazi oppression, compensation to American nisei for their incarceration during World War II, an excellent introductory work is Boris I. Bittker, *The Case for Black Reparations* (New York: Vintage Books, 1973). Appendix A is the "Black Reparations Manifesto"; Appendix B is "West German Reparations to Nazi Victims." Professor Bittker was in 1973 the Sterling Professor of Law at Yale University. This work provides analysis of the problems of compensating black Americans for damages inflicted upon them by segregation and the slave system; legal precedents; problems of international implications. The implications for applications in a transnational context are clear.

Black reparations is the only strategy proposed in discourse on the churches and deracization that (1) is an outcome of a theologically and scientifically sound definition of the human condition that is in extremis; (2) would follow logically from the churches' readiness to make amendment for their complicity in the protracted period of Christian racism in which all postcolonial churches are embroiled; (3) provides ecumenical churches prepared to repair the damage done to human community and Christian fellowship by racism with concrete and specific goals and methods for radical change that will move them into koinonia community; and (4) structures radical change in such a way that a new form of nonracial community is shaped by the norms of koinonia fellowship.

21. Professor Hacker's analysis of "white racism" in *Two Nations, Black and White,* is a useful "white" perspective for those who wish to understand the phenomenology of this condition.

22. *The New Delhi Report* (Geneva: World Council of Churches Publications, 1961). The World Council of Churches' position on this issue built on those taken by earlier organizations. The Third Assembly understood Christian unity in normative terms "all in each place" and "in every place." Bishop Lesslie Newbigin traces this theme's evolution in the article "Unity of 'All in Each Place,'" in *Dictionary of the Ecumenical Movement* (Geneva: World Council of Churches Publications, 1991), 1043–47. See Michael Kinnamon, ed., *Churches and the Christian World Communions,* Faith and Order Paper no. 118 (Geneva: World Council of Churches Publications, 1983), for use of New Delhi language on "allness."

14. A SHARING OF GIFTS AND STRUGGLES IN GOD'S WILL AND OUR UNITY

1. Michael Kinnamon, ed., *Signs of the Spirit: Official Report, Seventh Assembly* (Grand Rapids, Mich.: Eerdmans, 1991).

2. John Deschner, "Ecclesiological Aspects of the Race Problem," *International Review of Mission* 59 (1970): 293. Cf. also Dale T. Irvin, *Hearing Many Voices: Dialogue and Diversity in the Ecumenical Movement* (Lanham, Md.: University of America Press, 1994), 103.

3. Kortright Davis, *Can God Save the Church?* (St. Louis: Hodale Press, 1994).

4. William Watley, *Singing the Lord's Song in a Strange Land* (Geneva: World Council of Churches Publications, 1992). Cf. for more detailed treatment C. Eric Lincoln and Lawrence Mamiya, *The Black Church in the African American Experience* (Durham, N.C.: Duke University Press, 1990); Michael Harris, "African American Religious History in the 1980s: A Critical Review," *Religious Studies Review,* October 1994; Mary R. Sawyer, *Black Ecumenism: Implementing the Demands of Justice* (Valley Forge, Pa.: Trinity Press International, 1994).

5. Sawyer, *Black Ecumenism,* 3.

6. Alan Falconer, "Towards Unity through Diversity: Bilateral and Multilateral Dialogues," *One in Christ* 24, no. 4 (1993): 279–85.

7. Lukas Vischer, ed., *A Documentary History of the Faith and Order Movement: 1927–1963* (St. Louis: Bethany Press, 1963), 85. While this new Christocentric methodology has served the ecumenical movement well and produced such classical texts as "Scripture, Tradition and the Traditions" from Montreal in 1963 and "Baptism, Eucharist and Ministry" from Lima in 1982, it could marginalize the African American churches and African American scholars contributing to its process. However, as we look at the work of Randall Bailey, for example (e.g., *The Recovery of Black Presence: An Interdisciplinary Exploration,* edited with Jacquelyn Grant [Nashville: Abingdon Press, 1995]), disclosing the Eurocentric bias in much of biblical scholarship, or Thomas Hoyt (David T. Shannon and Gayraud Wilmore, eds., *Black Witness to the Apostolic Faith* [Grand Rapids, Mich.: Eerdmans, 1988]), disclosing the absence of the ethical implications of the public ministry of Jesus in the confessional use of the Christian Scriptures, we see that uniquely African American perspectives are essential correctives that come to life within the parameters of the Christocentric approach to ecumenical scripture scholarship. *Stony the Road We Trod,* ed. C. H. Felder (Minneapolis: Fortress Press, 1991), like parallel exegetical projects from

feminist, Asian, Latin American, and other contextual perspectives, points to the continuing durability, if further complexification, of this common approach to Scripture and the tradition.

8. Vischer, ed., *Documentary History*, 111.

9. Cf. P. C. Rodger and L. Vischer, *The Fourth World Conference on Faith and Order* (London: SCM, 1964).

10. Ibid.

11. Thomas Best, *On the Way to Fuller Koinonia* (Geneva: World Council of Churches Publications, 1994), 225.

12. Ibid., 232. In the discussion of common witness, there was an attempt to go beyond the recommendation of Lund for common action, to call for the churches to witness together in the world, where conscience did not require them to testify separately.

13. James Findlay, *Church People in the Struggle: The National Council of Churches and the Black Freedom Movement, 1950–1970* (New York: Oxford University Press, 1993).

14. Cf. Sawyer, *Black Ecumenism*. (Cf. note 21 below.)

15. In Jeffrey Gros and Joseph Burgess, eds., *Growing Consensus* (New York: Paulist Press, 1994), 9–96.

16. Ibid. "How can we have 'brotherhood' and 'sisterhood' without neighborhood?"

17. The struggle for civil rights in this country was rooted in the African American churches, and it became the greatest contribution of these churches to Christian unity in this century.

18. The U.S. African American churches find it difficult to help their people be enthusiastic about the National Council and local councils because of the racism they experience from Christian members of those churches.

19. Michael Kinnamon, *Truth and Community: Diversity and Its Limits in the Ecumenical Movement* (Grand Rapids, Mich.: Eerdmans, 1988).

20. Melva Costen, *African American Christian Worship* (Nashville: Abingdon Press, 1993).

21. Thomas F. Best, ed., "Report of the Harlem (1988) Consultation on the Unity and Renewal with Black Churches in the USA," *Midstream* (October 1989): 419.

22. This overview of Faith and Order work indicates the importance of the African American contribution to enhancing the texts put before the churches for their reconciliation, and of the dominant churches in the United States making a priority for listening to the African American voices contributing to the church's unity. The relationship of the Protestant and Roman Catholic churches within the African American community deserves specific attention.

23. The differences between the African American experience in the Roman Catholic and Protestant communities and the difference of ecumenical approaches need to be taken into account. The African American Catholic, whether in North, Central, or South America, will tend to view the Christian faith historically and ecclesiocentrically. The Roman Catholic Church, in a particular way, carries an important responsibility to repudiate the racist past of the church and to confess the sinfulness of racism among Christians, because it is the heir to the common pre-Reformation tradition of all of the

Western churches, and because it claims a universal ministry of reconciliation and a primacy, acknowledged in the West until the sixteenth century. Pope John Paul's confession and apology on the occasion of the Fifth Centenary (1992) are particularly important.

Protestants in North America and Catholics in Latin America will need to find ways of being sensitive to the differences of their experience and expectations in the ecumenical movement, in the African American, as in other Christian contexts.

APPENDIX: A GUIDE TO ADDRESS RACISM AND WORK FOR JUSTICE

1. Adapted from a guide written by Eleanor H. Haney in consultation with the Racial Justice Committee, Center for Vision and Policy, Box 89, HCR 63, Bath, ME 04530.

2. The following videos provide some resources for session I. They should be available from your local library or video store.

- *In Search of Our Fathers*—A film about a young man's search for his father after being raised by a strong, husbandless mother.
- *Promised Land: Montgomery, Alabama, Two Decades After Martin Luther King, Jr.*
- *Straight Up Rappin*—Documentary about the political and social realities of young rappers in New York.
- *Freedom Bags*—The story of African American women who moved from the rural South during the first three decades of the twentieth century.
- *Happy Birthday, Mrs. Craig*—Five generations of an African American family.

3. Peggy McIntosh, "White Privilege and Male Privilege: A Personal Account of Coming to See Correspondence through Work in Women's Studies," working paper no. 189 (Wellesley, Mass.: Wellesley College Center for Research on Women, 1988).

CONTRIBUTORS

RAYMOND STEVEN BLANKS is a lay minister in the Episcopal Church who directs the Emmaus Consulting Group, an ecumenical public policy and social advocacy organization in Washington, D.C. He also serves as the principal of the Ideal School of Washington, an inner-city independent high school.

REV. DR. SUSAN E. DAVIES is ordained in the United Church of Christ and serves on the faculty of Bangor Theological Seminary.

REV. DR. ARTHUR J. FREEMAN is a bishop in the Moravian Church in America and retired from the faculty of Moravian Theological Seminary, Bethlehem, Pennsylvania.

TEE GARLINGTON is a member of the International Evangelical Church, an evangelist in Atlanta, Georgia, and a staff member of Atlanta Metropolitan Cathedral.

BROTHER JEFFREY GROS, FSC, serves in the Secretariat for Ecumenical and Interreligious Affairs of the National Conference of Catholic Bishops.

ELEANOR HANEY is a member of the United Church of Christ and a former ethics professor at the Maine School of Art.

REV. DR. JACK W. HAYFORD is the pastor of the Church on the Way, Van Nuys, California.

SISTER PAUL TERESA HENNESSEE is a Sister of the Atonement and is an associate director of the Graymoor Ecumenical and Interreligious Institute, New York.

CHARLOTTE HOLLOMAN is a member of the Church of God in Christ and the director of the Beyond Racism Project in Milwaukee, Wisconsin.

DR. ALONZO JOHNSON is ordained in the Church of God in Christ and is on the faculty of Columbia Seminary, South Carolina.

REV. DR. RENA KAREFA-SMART is the former diocesan ecumenical officer, Episcopal Diocese of Washington, and is currently a priest associate designate in the Anglican Diocese of Freetown, Sierra Leone, Africa.

REV. DR. LEONARD LOVETT is the chief executive officer of Seminex Ministries.

REV. DEBORAH F. MULLEN is ordained in the Presbyterian Church and is on the faculty of McCormick Seminary, Chicago.

JACK MURTAUGH is a Roman Catholic and serves as the executive director of the Interfaith Conference of Greater Milwaukee.

ANNE P. SCHEIBNER is an Episcopalian who has served as staff to various national Episcopal and ecumenical projects.

LOUIS S. SCHOEN is an Episcopalian who retired in July 1998 as the director of the Commission on Life and Work of the Minnesota Council of Churches.

DR. GORDON E. TRUITT is the editor of *Pastoral Music* and the Catholic music educator for the National Association of Pastoral Musicians, Washington, D.C.